FRANCES R. CURCIO

MIO NONNO TOTORE
AND THE AMERICAN DREAM

This book is dedicated to

Nonno Totore's

great-great grandchildren,

and all those yet to come.

PAXTON THOMAS, 2015

VEDA ROSE, 2016

OWEN DECKER, 2016

CORDELIA ROSE, 2017

BODHI JAMES, 2018

SIENA CLAIRE, 2019

OLIVIA CATHERINE, 2022

MADELINE ROSE, 2024

Acknowledgements

It is said that "it takes a village." True to Italian tradition, I had a lot of support, encouragement, and love to guide and assist me throughout this research and writing project. This work could not have been developed or completed without the help of many kind and generous family members, dear friends, and professional acquaintances.

As I was piecing together this work, I reviewed many photos from family albums. *Hank* and *Robert Cipolaro* shared their family photos that helped me to construct some of the settings of our family history. *Robert* found and kindly gave me all the postcards that Nonno sent to his family in 1957 and 1962, during his visits to Italy. The postcards provided a wealth of information. Furthermore, right until the "last minute," before submitting this manuscript, I am grateful to Bob for answering several questions, and responding to my email messages expeditiously.

John Cipolaro also found in his late mother's collection, postcards written in 1957 and 1962 from Nonno. He made and gave me photocopies of them. One of the old postcards from 1962 motivated me to visit Lioni, and I initiated my search for relatives in Italy in 2012. John also generously provided views from his camera lens. Two of his special photos of Nonno appear in this manuscript.

Rosanne Denaro shared a treasure trove of photos and documents from her dear grandfather, Livio Cipolaro, Nonno's older brother. She accompanied me as we went to "scout out" 66 Mulberry Street, to see where our grandfathers spent their early years in America. Roe extended herself to share her memories and recollections of family events to help me piece together my Nonno's "story."

I

I am most grateful to master photographer *Giovanni D'Angelo,* who captured and shared images of Contursi-Terme and the statue of San Donato, included in this manuscript.

Danny Conroy, my electrician and gifted genealogist, was a great help in accessing and mining critical data from the Internet. *Alexandra Deluise*, former research librarian at Queens College, helped me to locate immigration documents. *Matthew Housch*, Archivist, Ellis Island Research Center, offered guidance and advice for locating immigration and naturalization documents.

Family photos and information related to Luigia, Nonno's only sister who came to America in the early 1900s to marry Oscar DeRosa, were kindly provided by her granddaughter, *Lois McGuire*. Dates and critical information required to construct the family tree, were provided by *Josephine Gallelli*, granddaughter of Livio Cipolaro. The *late Marlene Guiamano* and her daughter *Tara DeLucia*, descendants of Tullio Cipollaro, Nonno's youngest brother, who also settled in America, kindly shared their family data.

Tony Troiano, Orazio Fotografik, a talented restorative photographer and graphic designer, has been a constant resource since 2013, when he restored the "Cipollaro Brothers Tailors" photograph. He has since restored other family photographs and he designed two versions of my family tree. The full version fills a large wall in my house. The "truncated" version appears in this manuscript.

I am indebted to authors who have graciously shared their helpful advice and opinions related to the development of this manuscript. I extend my gratitude to *Raymond Angelo Belliotti*, author of *Values, Virtues and Vices Italian Style*, among other works; *Helene Stapinski*, author of *Murder in Matera*, among other works; and *Sophia Romero*, author of *Always Hiding*. Queens College Professor Emerita *Myra Zarnowski* kindly reviewed early versions of this manuscript and offered invaluable advice.

Since Nonno was a tailor, I did not want to leave any "stone unturned" related to his profession. I came across a reference to *The Tailor's Thread*, by Vincent Rocco Saladini, Sr. After extensive searching, I was unsuccessful in locating a copy of the book. Fortunately, by persevering, I was able to locate and contact the author's daughter, *Deborah Massaro.* She generously and kindly sent me an autographed copy of her father's heartwarming autobiography.

Mariano Cipollaro, my third cousin, is an amazing Contoursian historian. He recently retired from the Contursi Municipio. He has been instrumental in providing essential documents, books, and personal anecdotes to support my research.

Philip Boffa, a classic car specialist, assisted in determining the year and the make of my Nonno's Dodge car in an old photograph, included in this manuscript.

Richard Cipolaro, the eldest of Nonno's grandchildren, listened to and commented on many of the stories that I remembered, and he added some of his own memories. *Ralph Curcio,* my brother and the youngest of Nonno's grandsons, helped to clarify some of the stories.

My very dear friends in Salerno, Italy, *Mary D'Ambrosio* and *Gaetana Sessa* were always ready to offer assistance in obtaining, translating, interpreting, and explaining documents to "unlock" access to important information.

Isabella DePiero, my former seventh-grade science teacher, has always been supportive and positive as she listened to my stories and offered advice. She kindly accompanied me on many of my "searches."

Last but not least, I must recognize my dear cousin *Joanne Maruffi* who has put up with me throughout the many years it has taken to bring this project to fruition. She has been my "sounding board"— always ready to listen, and offer support, advice, and wise words of encouragement.

I have tried to be true to the historical facts and details available. I take full responsibility for any inaccuracies or inconsistencies.

Foreword

A found postcard sent from Lioni, Italy to Staten Island, NY in 1962 combined with a chance encounter in 2012 with a second cousin in the region where her grandfather Salvatore—*Totore* —Cipollaro— was born sets the stage for Frances Curcio's quest to learn about and document the life of her beloved grandfather Nonno Totore. In the following pages, Curcio takes us on this rich journey with her and with him as she speculates and reimagines his life: his austere childhood in Contursi Terme in southern Italy, the arduous crossing he and over a million Italian immigrants made to Ellis Island in 1904 when he was fourteen, his years in Manhattan's Little Italy where he worked tirelessly as an apprentice tailor during the day, learned English at night, and married and started a family, and then the more prosperous years of realizing the American Dream—having a house built on the north shore of Staten Island, being chosen to make suits for General Dwight D. Eisenhower, Pierre S. duPont, Horace Dodge, and Babe Ruth. But Curcio doesn't begin with the span of these years. She begins with his retirement—the twenty-two years he lived with her and her parents after her grandmother, his wife Ettora, passed away—years she remembers vividly and joyfully. She recalls this time until his death as "easy, fun, and carefree," the opposite of the kind of journey it had taken him to get there.

One wouldn't know from Salvatore the conditions he lived in as a young boy or how deplorable steerage was on the steamship *S.S. Sardegna* or the hardships of tenement living, and this is, in part, Curcio's point. The qualities she loves most about her grandfather are his humility, endurance and reticence. Her only regret is that she didn't

V

ask him the questions she meant to ask while he was alive. Yet if she had, or if he had offered them to her, this would be a different book. It's her questions, her reaching for answers, her research, and her speculation—what was it like for him to be one of ten children, to leave his parents and all he knew behind at such a young age, to acclimate to a country that was not his own, that did not always welcome him?—that give the tone of this work both its urgency and its tenderness. She says it's his untold story that motivated her to tell it, and she does so by weaving autobiography, family history, historical research, photos, and even, in the appendix, instructions for *scopa* and *briscola*, "brisk," two Neapolitan card games that she enjoyed playing with her Nonno Totore. This is the grandfather whose gifted precision as a custom tailor helped lead her—his only granddaughter—to her future career as an accomplished professor of mathematics education, whose love and attention contributed to her success in the study of Italian, and whose strong moral and spiritual center helped her to thrive like the young maple tree he taught her father how to plant in the front yard.

Readers will not only appreciate the poignant discoveries and memories Curcio shares of her grandfather but will also learn, or be reminded of, the enormous sacrifices and victories experienced by so many of his culture and generation. They—*you*—will find yourself admiring both this grandfather and this granddaughter whose gratitude for her grandfather and for finding answers to his life is unmistakable. You'll be glad she embarked on this act of love—the many return visits she made to Italy, the many familial and scholarly sources she consulted, the many cherished memories she sorted through in the eleven years she spent researching and writing this book. You'll be glad she looked out the same window Salvatore looked out from in Contursi Terme more than a hundred years earlier and imagined what he saw, imagined all that lay ahead.

— **MARIA GIURA PHD**
Author of *Celibate: A Memoir*
and *What My Father Taught Me*

Table of Contents

Preface	1
Life with Nonno	11
Life in Contursi-Terme	35
Leaving Contursi-Terme	45
Life in Steerage	51
Approaching the Statue of Liberty	55
Arriving at Ellis Island	59
Making a Living, Composing a Life	63
Realizing the American Dream	77
"Questa è la Fine"	83
Selected Bibliography	85
Family Tree	92
Appendices	
1: Map of Contursi	94
2: Nonno's Birth certificate	100
3: Nonno's Naturalization Papers	102
4: Nonni's Marriage Certificate	105
5: Scopa and Scopone	106
6: Briscola	108

Preface

"…you're going through life,
you have this trajectory and this vision,
then suddenly this whole other good
thing is like a sidecar attached to you,
and you're off in another direction."
— STANLEY TUCCI[1]

Writing this book has been a true labor of love. For most of my academic and professional life I have focused on the teaching and learning of mathematics and preparing mathematics teachers. I loved every minute of it. But now, I am charting new waters.

Although I grew up knowing that I am Italian/American and my dear immigrant grandfather, *Nonno* Salvatore, also known as *Totore*, lived with my family for twenty-two years after *Nonna* Ettorina, my grandmother, died, interest in my Italian heritage did not develop until 2011, when I was sixty years old. I planned to celebrate this milestone with a visit with my family to Nonno's hometown, Contursi-Terme in Southern Italy. Before going, I wanted to know a little bit about it, its location and how to get there. I checked on a map of Italy, and I found it located on Monte di Pruno, a volcanic mountain in southwestern Italy. I read online that Contursi is in the Province of Salerno in the Region of Campania (see map in Appendix 1). I calculated that it is about 108 km (67 miles) southeast of Naples, taking approximately 1.5 hours by car

---

1.   Marshall, "Passion for Acting Shifts to Food," p. C2.

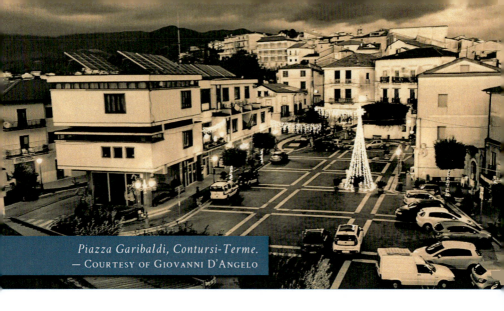

Piazza Garibaldi, Contursi-Terme.
— Courtesy of Giovanni D'Angelo

from Naples. I learned that its name could have originated from the Latin "cum turris," meaning "with tower." I made a note to be on the lookout for a tower. Another source suggested that "Contursi" was derived from the name of the feudal lord, prince of Salerno, Count Orso, who established the village, and built his castle in the year 840[2]. What I also found interesting was that Contursi was the site of major Parkinson's Disease research in the late 1990s. The researchers found a preponderance of genetic markers among Contursi kindred, sixty individuals spanning five generations[3]. Reading about this triggered my memory to my uncle's mother-in-law who was from Contursi and afflicted with Parkinson's Disease. I wondered whether this genetic marker could be present in my family. So as not to put a damper on my excitement to travel to Contursi, I saved this thought for another time.

I hired Pasquale, a driver and translator. He picked up my relatives and me at our hotel in Sorrento and drove us to the small town where Nonno Totore was born. After driving about 90 minutes, we arrived on Via Sottotenente and drove right to Piazza Garibaldi, the main square in the old section of the commune, named after the famous Italian liberator, Giuseppe Garibaldi. The piazza, a large open area, is surrounded

---

2. Borzellino *Contursi Terme*; F. Pignata, *Il Sentiero*; V. Pignata, *Contursi Terme*; Regione, *Contursi Terme*.

3. Golbe et al., "Clinical Genetic Analysis;" "The Contursi Kindred."

by typical Southern Italian stone houses and buildings of similar color clustered together, and a small bar. During Nonno's childhood years the piazza may have been the place for outdoor town meetings, improvisational entertainment, and perhaps the broadcasting of news by the *banditore*, the town crier. We walked along some unpaved narrow pathways. We were very excited when we found ourselves on a paved pathway named "Via Boffa," the family name of one of my aunts, whose sons were journeying with me. Visiting this small, charming commune with its "old world" flavor, had a profound effect on me.

We entered the *Municipio* and went to the office where birth, death, and marriage records are kept. Pasquale helped us to communicate with Signora Lenza, the office administrator. Knowing Nonno's birthdate made it easy for her to locate his birth certificate in one of the tomes arranged by year on the shelf.

Signora Lenza carefully pulled a large record book off the shelf. It was dated 1890. I was very surprised that while flipping through the pages she did not wear gloves to protect the magnificently scripted, delicately aged pages from the oils of her fingers. She quickly located the birth record of Nonno (see Appendix 2). I was overwhelmed with emotion upon seeing his birth certificate. My eyes welled up as I tried to read the lengthy text in Italian. I grabbed my camera to take a picture of the page to study the text at a later time. Mrs. Lenza also showed us the birth certificates of Nonno's brother Livio, whom I knew, and a sister, Battilda, whom I never knew.

After visiting Contursi and other sites in Southern Italy, my family and I returned home, some of us to New York, others to Massachusetts. Although we did not meet any living relatives and we could not find any relatives buried in the cemetery in Contursi, we believed that the trip fulfilled our desire to see the place that Nonno often spoke about when we were all very young and gathered around the dinner table on special occasions.

Later that summer, my dear Aunt Virginia passed away, leaving a lot of memorabilia. Her son John kindly gave me copies of the postcards that Nonno sent to his family in 1957 and 1962, when he returned to

Italy as an American citizen. One of the postcards written in 1962, was sent from Lioni. I had never heard of this place. I do not recall Nonno speaking about Lioni. So, I looked it up on a map of Italy and I saw that it is located not too far from Contursi.

The following year, I planned my next trip to Italy to visit Lioni. When I showed my driver/translator Pasquale the postcard (see photo of postcard below), he told me that I may be disappointed because in 1980 there was a devastating earthquake measuring 6.9 on the Richter scale that destroyed many of the homes in the small towns near Contursi. Lioni was one of them. It did not matter to me; I was determined to see the town. When we arrived, we found the defunct train station and the street with the houses that had been rebuilt that were depicted on the postcard. We walked around and decided to go to the *Municipio*

Postcard of Lioni, 1962.

Mio Nonno Totore and The American Dream

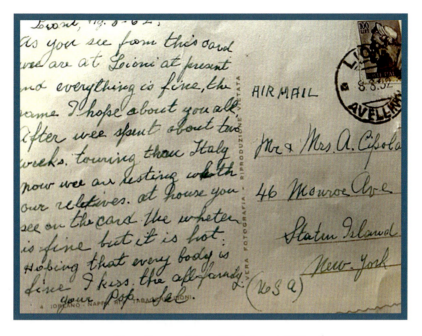

Text of postcard from Lioni, August 1962, indicating Nonno's relatives' house is on the postcard.

to ask about relatives. The clerk found the pink death card of Cristina Cipollaro Carfagna, whose parents, Alfonso and Margherita, were also the parents of my Nonno. Although she died in 1958, I found Nonno's oldest sister!

I asked Pasquale to take me to the cemetery where we found the Carfagna mausoleum and crypts that had photos of the deceased. Two of the names, Margherita and Amedeo, were familiar to me because my mother was Margherita and her brother, my uncle, was Amedeo. And I found one of my great aunts, Florinda, whose nameless picture taken in 1944 with my Uncle Henry serving in the U. S. Army, I had with me (see next page). My heart was pumping with disbelief and excitement.

After visiting the cemetery, we returned to the scene on the postcard. An elderly man approached us and, speaking in Italian, asked whether he could be of any help. Pasquale told him that I was from America looking for *famiglia Carfagna*. His eyes widened and

*Henry Cipolaro posing with his Aunt Florinda Cipollaro,
Contursi-Terme, January 1944.
— Cipolaro/Curcio Family Album*

excitedly announced that his wife is a Carfagna. I was extremely surprised. I wondered: how could this be? This stranger in this little remote town has a wife who may be a member of the family I was seeking. He invited us in. His wife, Lina, a short but imposing and strong woman, questioned me—*Chi sei?* (Who are you?) I showed her the postcard from

Mio Nonno Totore and The American Dream

1962 and told her Totore was *mio Nonno*. At that point, we all started to cry. Since this meeting, except during the Covid pandemic, I have been visiting my newly found family members, trying to piece together our family tree and our history that all started in Contursi.

The early trips motivated me to investigate and write about my family roots described in several articles in my local newspaper, *The Staten Island Advance*, listed in the bibliography[4]. I obtained and reviewed family documents, including the manifest of the steamship, *Sardegna*, that Nonno took in 1904, when he was fourteen years old. Despite the negative opinions and attitudes towards immigrants from Southern Italy, he was sent to the New World by his father to join his older brother, Livio. I have often wondered what Nonno's father knew about the New World, and what were his expectations for his young son? Was he aware that Italians were being "swindled to New York"[5]? Was he concerned that the Italians were not welcome in America[6]? What was it like for Nonno to leave his family, never to see his parents and some of his siblings ever again? Was he resentful? Nonno never shared his thoughts about leaving his family. I wonder whether Nonno was given a choice to leave or to stay, but most likely, in the strict patriarchal Italian tradition, his father ordered him to go. So, Nonno emigrated from Italy embarking on a journey to, as he would say, "*l'America.*" How difficult this must have been for a fourteen-year-old. I am in awe of what Nonno must have endured, how much he achieved in his lifetime, and the foundation he established for his children and their future. His untold story motivated me to share it as an expression of my great admiration, love, and respect.

This new-found interest in family history became my "sidecar," and it has taken me in a new and exciting direction. What follows is the result of many years of research in reconstructing Nonno's life and

---

4. See Benanti, "Digging Deeper;" Curcio, "Island Family Sets Off," "Arrochar Resident,"; Sherry, "Grassroots Research."

5. Tucciarone and Lariccia, *Italians Swindled.*

6. Stapinski, "When America Barred Italians."

his fulfillment of the American Dream. In the last ten years, I have often thought about and regretted why I never asked Nonno the many questions I have that would have made writing his story easy. I have tried to fill in the gaps in my knowledge by reading many books, visiting Ellis Island numerous times, and watching some old Italian movies to help me answer my questions. I read Italian/American literature, both nonfiction and fiction. I was greatly influenced by a course at Queens College of the City University of New York that I audited in the fall 2020, *Studies in Italian American Literature*, taught by Distinguished Professor Fred Gardaphé. At this time, I became familiar with the beautiful, sensitive words of Joseph Tusiani and Robert Viscusi, some of which I have cited to help me capture the essence of the messages that I try to convey in different parts of my Nonno's story. I also enrolled in several excellent, inspiring virtual writing-your-Italian memories workshops offered by author, Dr. Maria Giura, through Casa Belvedere, on Staten Island. I am grateful to her for reviewing earlier versions of this work and offering advice. I am honored that she accepted my invitation to write the "Foreword."

My Nonno's story may seem like it is from Horatio Alger's late nineteenth-century collection of stories of respectful, honest, industrious adolescent boys who through hard work and perseverance rise from rags to riches, as they look at life optimistically.[7] My Nonno epitomized the characteristics of many Italian immigrants. As a young and impressionable adolescent, he exemplified "*courage, perseverance*, and *exploration*."[8] Through my recollection of living with my Nonno for twenty-two years, until his death in 1974, his story reflects his considerate, kind, and astute character. He provided an exemplary role model for his children and grandchildren. I hope to reveal why I believe that he was an extraordinary embodiment of the American Dream. Being a humble and modest man, what follows may not be the story that my Nonno would have wanted me to tell, but it is my best attempt at telling his story as authentically as possible.

---

7. Algier, *The Collected Complete Work*.

8. Tamburri, *The Columbus Affair*, p. 29; original in italics.

Overview

His story starts with what is most familiar and memorable to me in the section "Life with Nonno." After an extensive amount of research and reading, I conjectured about what his life must have been like in Contursi-Terme, and what he probably endured in steerage on his way to America. "Approaching the Statue of Liberty," "Arriving at Ellis Island," and tenement living are all preludes to "Making a Living, Composing a Life," and my interpretation of Nonno's "Realization of the American Dream." The "Afterword: Questa è la Fine," is really not an ending, but rather, a continuation of Nonno's influence in the lives of his progeny.

Nonno Salvatore "Totore" Cipolaro, taken in the late 1960s.
— Courtesy of John K. Cipolaro.

Life With Nonno

"Thinking back now, I really must say
I feel lucky and privileged to have known Grandpa to this day.
For in my life, [he has] played a special part.
The memories I will treasure and keep close to my heart."
— ILONA M. BLAKE[9]

When we first met, my Nonno Totore was 61 years old, and I was a newborn. After he and Nonna welcomed two grandsons into the family, I was the first, and as it turns out after three more grandsons arrived, the only granddaughter, a daughter of his only daughter. He always told me that I was his "favorite" granddaughter. I was probably about six years old when I realized that I had no competition, and I retorted, "But I am your *only* granddaughter!" We laughed.

Before I was born and during my very early years, my parents lived with Nonno and Nonna. When Nonna Ettorina died in 1952, my father started building our new house on the corner property adjacent to Nonno's house. We all moved into the new house in 1954, the year my brother was born. Nonno lived with us until 1974, the year he died. During the time he was with us, I remember that life was easy, fun, and carefree. My earliest recollection of Nonno was when I was about three years old, watching him peel a tangerine—his favorite fruit. He taught me the name of the fruit, but I couldn't pronounce it, so I called it "verneen." He didn't mind, he just laughed with me. He would sit me on his lap and give me sections of the fruit to eat. It became my

---

9.   Blake, *Family Friend Poems.*

favorite fruit, too. To this day, every time I peel a tangerine (yes, I say it correctly now), I think of this special time with Nonno.

Throughout my early years, every morning I would watch how Nonno used a funny-shaped curved knife to wedge out fresh grapefruit sections after cutting the grapefruit in half with a regular knife. He would eat half of it one day and save the other half for the next day. He would then peel the skin of an orange and eat the orange slices, too. He loved citrus fruits, and I, too, acquired a taste and a love for them. He heated a cup of milk with a little bit of coffee and crushed two Nabisco Graham crackers in the cup. This was his "continental breakfast." He did this consistently at about 7 AM every day. Although he was a retired custom tailor, I remember him around the house being dressed impeccably, sometimes even wearing a tie. He always seemed to be on a schedule. I cannot believe that to this day, I, too, follow a schedule, but I do not wear a tie.

What impressed me was that Nonno was always very considerate, pensive, and jovial. I observed how he was respectful and kind to everyone. He was supportive and shared his opinions, but he never interfered with typical family issues. He was somewhat aloof, not wanting to be "in the way," and he never was. Although he never told me, I believe his behavior and personality developed from experiences during his life as a child, when he was the eighth of ten siblings living in rural Contursi-Terme. I wonder, what was it like to be in a family with ten children? Did his siblings protect him or pick on him? Another experience that may have shaped his behavior and personality was when he was only fourteen years old, on his way to America on the steamship *Sardegna*. What was it like to endure horrific, crowded conditions in steerage? Did he feel lonely even though he was always among a horde of people? During his early stay in America, Nonno lived in a crowded, suffocating room in a tenement building. What was it like to live in such inhumane conditions? What were his coping strategies? No wonder Nonno never spoke about his early experiences at home, at sea, and in the New World. His personality, attitudes, and behaviors evolved by learning how to cope. Like many of his peers, he survived and took advantage of positive, productive ways to compose a life and carve out his own special space and place in his new surroundings.

Nonno wisely used the principle of teaching by example as a means for establishing a foundation for building a strong work ethic among his family. He worked hard and he was frugal. Obviously, he had adapted to the "American way." Although I believe that he had high expectations for his children, unlike his father who determined Nonno's profession as a tailor, Nonno supported his sons as they chose their careers. He was strict but in a gentle way. Unlike many of his Southern Italian immigrant peers who brought "antischool bias with them,"[10] Nonno valued education because he realized that, in America, education would be the key to success. So, after high school his sons attended business school. They worked themselves up from office boys to successful businessmen. Although it was not common among Italian immigrants at the time, I believe that Nonno would have supported his daughter's wish to attend college to become a teacher, but as a teenager she became ill and was unable to complete high school. Fulfilling not only my dream, but my mother's dream as well, I became the teacher.

My mother told me that her mother, Nonna Ettorina, said that Nonno was *un santo*, a "saint." To make such a proclamation, he must have been a wonderful husband and father. I always noticed that he never yelled, he never became angry, he was kind, generous, and helpful. His days on earth were punctuated by the feast days of *due santi*, two saints: St. Valentine and St. Blaise. Every February 14th, the feast day of St. Valentine, a second-century priest who risked his life by defying Emperor Claudius II and marrying young couples in love, my family would celebrate Nonno's birthday. His daughter, Margherita, named after his mother, would make his favorite strawberry shortcake from "scratch." The day of love was a perfect day for Nonno to enter the world.

---

10. Gambino, *Blood of my Blood*, p. 252.

February birthday celebrations at Bisnonna Antoinetta's house. From left to right: Cousins Annagrace (Feb. 25), Antoinetta, and Margherita; Bisnonna (Feb. 28); Zia Filomena; Nonno Totore (Feb. 14); Zia Maria, and Henry. Circa 1954; from the Vece/Maruffi Family Album.

Dying on Sunday, February 3rd was also meaningful. Naturally, I was extremely upset after hearing that Nonno had died. I sought consolation by attending mass and praying for Nonno. It was not until I attended mass on this day that I became familiar with the feast of St. Blaise, Bishop and Martyr. After mass, the priest used two crossed candles to bless the throats of those who approached the altar to receive the benediction. This symbolizes the saint's power for healing afflictions of the throat. Every year on this day, I sponsor a mass in memory of Nonno. As a tailor since he was a child, Nonno inhaled fabric fibers and as a result, as he aged, he developed emphysema. He frequently coughed and he always had *muco*, phlegm. Although he did not die from emphysema, to remember Nonno on the Feast of St. Blaise not only commemorates the day he passed, but it also brings attention to his profession that caused his respiratory malady.

Returning to Italy

In December 1956, I recall a veil of sadness descending upon our typically joyous Christmas dinner, when Nonno announced that he and his older brother Livio were planning a trip to Contursi because one of their older sisters had died in March. It would be their first time returning to their hometown since they emigrated more than fifty years ago. I was very young, sitting around the table with my young cousins and my baby brother, trying to understand what was casting such sadness among Nonno, my parents, aunts, and uncles. It was not the first time we had heard of Contursi. Nonno used to talk about his hometown all the time. Unlike adults who left their hometown after accumulating vivid memories over the years, it is surprising what he

Nonno Totore with grandchildren Robert and Henry Jr., brother Livio, son Henry Sr., nephew Nino, and friends before boarding the ocean liner Augustus.
— Cipolaro/Curcio Family Album

remembered, since he was sent to America when he was young. It was obviously an ample amount of time for him to develop an emotional attachment. He never had the chance to see his parents before they died. His father died in 1918, and his mother died in 1934. Since 1904, he had also not seen six of his siblings who had remained in Italy. Now, he and *Zio* Livio, Uncle Livio, were planning to go back because the property where their sister lived belonged to their family, and it had to be sold. According to Italian law and tradition, the oldest male heir, Livio, was responsible to sign the documents. In addition to tending to the family business, Nonno and Zio Livio planned a 15-day motorcoach tour of Italy.

In 1957, when spring arrived, there were a lot of preparations for Nonno's trip. As an American citizen since 1922, he had to apply for a United States passport. He had to purchase ocean liner tickets. His son Henry and his family gifted Nonno with two beautiful suitcases. Nonno had to be sure he had enough medication. Did he need any special clothing, comfortable shoes, and personal grooming items for the trip?

The ocean liner, Augustus.
— Cipolaro/Curcio Family Album)

Mio Nonno Totore and The American Dream

Preparing to return to Italy was a lot different from when he left Italy 53 years prior. His two new suitcases that he called *valigie*, valises, had to be filled with his clothes and gifts for his oldest sister, Cristina, his nieces and nephews, and his great nieces. When the day of departure arrived, we all went to the pier in Manhattan to wish Nonno and Zio Livio a *buon viaggio*. In those days, guests were permitted to board the ship, visit the cabin, sit in a dining room, and sip champagne. My brother, cousins, and I were too young to drink champagne, so Nonno bought us soda to join in the *buon viaggio* toast. It was very exciting to be aboard an ocean liner and to see where Nonno would "live" during his voyage.

The ocean liner, the *Augustus*, was a very large, modern, and beautiful ship built in 1950. I wonder whether Nonno was thinking about how very different the conditions were from his time in steerage when he emigrated to America. It must have been difficult not to make comparisons. He never shared his impressions, and I never thought to ask. Of course, the costs of passage were much different (e.g., 15,000 lire, about $30 for steerage in the early 1900s vs. $220 on average per person, double occupancy, for tourist class on an ocean liner in the mid-1950s).[11]

During Nonno's time in Italy, he religiously kept in touch with all of us, writing and sending many postcards, sharing his itinerary, impressions, and health, and asking about the family. He was always sure to send his love to his grandchildren. In some postcards he wrote that he was happy to receive letters from his children sent to the home of relatives in Lioni. (These were the very postcards that surfaced 54 years after they had been written and saved by my late Aunts Virginia and Mildred.) When he returned home in September, there was a "welcome home" gathering. Nonno showered everyone with souvenirs, and he enthusiastically shared his special memories. He remembered that I was preparing for my First Holy Communion, so he brought me rosary beads from the Vatican. This special gift is a continued reminder of how Nonno blessed my life.

---

11. $30 in 1904 is about $1,010 in 2023 dollars. $220 in 1957 is about $2,345 in 2023 dollars.

Nonno returned to Italy five years later with Zio Livio and Arturo, a friend of theirs. His oldest sister, Cristina, died, and they went to pay their respects to her family. They left New York City en route to Naples, embarking on an 8-day journey on the luxurious ocean liner, the Leonardo da Vinci, built in 1960. Cristina's son Amedeo and his family hosted Nonno, Zio Livio, and Arturo, in Lioni. The three widowers also spent time in Salerno. I recall Nonno saying that Salerno was his favorite city—clean and quiet. The water was calm for swimming.

Before Nonno's 1962 trip leaving from the cruise port in New York City. From left to right: Richard, Frances, Nonno, Ralph, and John; June 1962.
— Cipollaro/Curcio Family Album

The ocean liner, Leonardo da Vinci.

From left to right: Nonno Totore, Zio Livio, and Arturo, dining on the Leonardo Da Vinci en route to Naples; 1962.

Frances R. Curcio

In the mid-1950s, after retiring as a custom tailor and moving in my family's house, my father helped Nonno create a workshop in the basement, where he continued to make suits for his sons, my father, and other men. He would also alter and embellish garments for many friends and family members, for both men and women. When I did not have to go to school, I used to sit and watch him measure twice and cut once. I never realized that he was "bilingual" in measurements, first learning the metric system of measurement when he was an apprentice tailor to his father in Contursi. In 1861, when Italy became unified, the metric system became the official system of measure. Then, as a custom tailor in the United States, Nonno had to master the English standard system of measure. He had many rulers and tape measures that I enjoyed using to practice my measuring skills. This early experience developed my appreciation for the precision and usefulness of mathematics.

Nonno's "shop" had a commercial Singer sewing machine set up on a table with a treadle for his feet to control the motion and speed of the needle. Although the treadle could function without electricity, Nonno had his sewing machine connected to an electrical outlet. The machine had dials and levers to adjust the size of the stitches. Nonno used a variety of tools. I had no idea that there were so many different sizes of shears and needles used for different purposes. There were boxes of pins, needles, thimbles, and assorted colors of thread, all available at his fingertips. As a very young apprentice in Contursi, most likely he had to manage and organize all the tools of the trade, and he maintained the same system for his work as a custom tailor.

One day I watched Nonno working on a suit to be made with fabric designed with pin stripes. I recall that he told me that fabrics with stripes and geometric designs are the most difficult to work with because careful planning and measuring were essential to ensure that the stripes or designs were properly aligned from the shoulders to the sleeves, and the overlay of the pockets on the front of the jacket had to align with the fabric to which they were attached.

Nonno told me that you can judge the skill of a tailor by how precisely the stripes are aligned. I observed how Nonno was a master at this, and to this day, I am very attentive to this quality of men's and women's suits.

When I was in the fifth grade, girls were required to take sewing. I was happy to learn how to sew so I could work like Nonno. For one project, we had to make a gingham apron. Nonno gave me the red checkered fabric to bring to school, where we learned how to use a pattern to design and create the apron. We also learned how to use pinking shears. We started the project in school and then we were assigned to complete the apron at home. I was lucky because Nonno supervised my work. He guided my little fingers in using shears, pinning seams, threading needles, making sure I wore a thimble that I often resisted wearing, working with bias seam binding, basting and then, operating my mother's portable Singer sewing machine. I was so proud of my final product and what I learned that I still wear my apron when I work in the kitchen. I continue to make use of my valuable sewing skills to this day by mending, adjusting, and embellishing garments and fabric home goods.

Gingham apron made over sixty years ago.

Wise Words

Whenever an opportunity to teach a lesson presented itself, Nonno took advantage of the moment. One Friday night in the fall of 1961, when my mother was in the hospital recuperating from an operation, Nonno, my father, my brother, and I were invited to have dinner at the house of my mother's dear cousin Antoinette and her family. Antoinette thoroughly enjoyed cooking and entertaining—no, she *loved* cooking and entertaining. She was robust, jolly, and fun-loving. She put her whole heart into her cooking. The table was set for eight people—four in her family and four in my family. As usual in Antoinette's house, the aroma was overwhelmingly delicious. The flavors of her rich gravy seeped into our nostrils. The fried chicken cutlets were steaming and oozing. I was sitting next to Nonno. When Antoinette placed the chicken cutlets on the table, with my soft, 10-year-old voice, I whispered into Nonno's ear, "But Nonno, today is Friday, we can't eat meat." Knowing and appreciating the hard work that went into preparing the elaborate dinner, Nonno drew me close to him and hugged me saying, "Remember, it's not what goes in your mouth, it's what comes out of it." At that point, I felt God wouldn't mind if I ate the chicken...I hope not. It was more than 60 years later, while attending a weekday mass that I heard an echo of Nonno's voice as I listened to the Gospel according to St. Matthew. Jesus was chastising the scribes and Pharisees to teach a lesson: "Not what goes into the mouth defiles a man; but what comes out of the mouth, this defiles a man" (15:11). I wonder whether Nonno was aware that he was paraphrasing scripture? I am sure I heard this passage from St. Matthew many times, but maybe I never listened carefully to make the connection.

One day, Nonno was helping my father plant a maple tree in front of our house. They inserted wood and tied the tree to the wood to stabilize it and to keep it straight. I asked them why they had to do that. Nonno said that a young tree is like a young child. It must be supported to grow straight because once it grows crooked, it cannot be straightened out. Many years later I found a related quotation from

St. Frances Xavier Cabrini, the patron saint of immigrants, who said, "How arduous is the work of setting on the right path those who have gone astray"[12] I do not know whether Nonno was aware of this quotation, but I do know that Nonno was a very wise and thoughtful man.

At the supper table one night my family discussed lying and telling the truth. The discussion was motivated by hearing that one of our middle school friends had gotten into trouble for lying and he was caught. Of course, part of the discussion emphasized that it is a sin to tell a lie. But Nonno also added some advice. He said, "Remember, when you tell the truth, you don't have to remember what you said." I added this to my list of wise advice from Nonno.

Italian Music

Nonno loved to listen to Italian music on the radio; perhaps it was opera. It was not until more than 50 years later, that I learned that Nonno's favorite Italian song was "Chella Là." I do not remember Nonno singing or dancing, except when he danced with me at my parents' surprise 25th wedding anniversary in 1973 (see photo on the back cover).

As a child, I remember sitting in the living room with Nonno and my family on Saturday nights watching the Lawrence Welk Show. I was particularly interested in watching and listening to accordionist Myron Floren. From the time I was five years old, I wanted *una fisarmonica*, an accordion, so I could play like Myron Floren. Dating back to its development in Austria in 1828, the accordion found its way throughout European party and concert venues[13]. I learned that it was very popular in 20th-century Italy. Why it was the accordion that attracted my attention, I really do not know. I found the slightly off-pitch musette tone to be very charming and melodic. It could convey

---

12. Cabrini, *To the Ends of the Earth*, p. 251.

13. Jacobson, *Squeeze This!*

feelings of joy as well as sorrow. Italian music played on an accordion had such a big influence on me that I wanted to make music, to be the provider of happy sounds and reminiscences. No one believed that a five-year-old could be sure of what she wanted, so I kept nagging until I was twelve years old, and my dream finally came true. In 1963, Nonno helped my parents buy my first accordion and I began music lessons. All these years later, I am so grateful for having had the experience that the gift of music brings happiness for a lifetime. Once I was able to play Italian songs, I know Nonno and my parents enjoyed listening and humming along. I remember practicing in the kitchen while my mother cooked dinner and Nonno sat at the table. I hope Nonno enjoyed listening to my rendition of "Chella Là."

Playing Cards

Every Sunday afternoon after dinner, Nonno would walk down McClean Avenue, to visit his brothers-in-law and play *Briscola,* an Italian card game (see Appendix 6 for rules of the game). Nonno called the game "Brisk," but it is translated as "trump." Whenever I had the chance to stop by, I would hear the loud bantering among the men, sometimes angry that the cards were not the ones needed to win. But it was all in fun.

In my house, card playing spilled over after dinner each night, when as a preadolescent, I would play the Neapolitan card game *Scopa* with Nonno (see Appendix 5 for the rules of the game). At the time, always emphasizing English meanings, Nonno told me the name of the card game was "Sweep." It was not until many years later when I visited my newly found cousin Lina in Lioni, that I learned the Italian name of the game—*Scopa,* to sweep up like a broom.

Before playing cards, I helped my parents clean the dishes and the kitchen while Nonno finished reading the local newspaper, *The Staten Island Advance.* Although we did not have a Neapolitan deck of cards, Nonno removed the 8s, 9s, and 10s, so the standard 52-card deck was reduced to a 40-card deck. Years later, my cousin Lina introduced me to the Neapolitan deck of 40 cards containing ten cards in each of four suits: *denari, spade, bastoni, coppe* (i.e., coins, swords, batons, and cups). She helped me to recall the rules of the game and I told her how I used to play with Nonno, her great uncle. Lina also explained how to play *Scopone*, a variation of *Scopa* for four players instead of two.

I noticed that as Nonno aged, his hands would shake a lot while he held the cards. He always asked me to shuffle the cards. I wondered, why did his hands shake? Was he nervous? He didn't seem to be. We talked about the cards while we played but I never asked him about his shaky hands. Sometimes I would make a silly move and Nonno would ask me if I really wanted to do that. I would give him a hug and then re-do the play. I didn't feel as though our playing was competitive, we were having fun, and he was teaching me strategies. Whenever Nonno corrected my playing, I would win. When he saw that I was happy, he would laugh.

Nonno also taught me how to play Italian solitaire. We would use the 40-card deck, and systematically reveal each card, appropriately placing it in one of the four columns, moving cards to align with their proper suits and situating them in the proper numerical order. Nonno let me play first and he quietly watched what I would do with the cards. Playing solitaire was not difficult. Nonno was a good teacher and I tried to be a good student. These times together were precious and memorable.

Language Learning

Although Nonno's education was limited to a few years in Contursi and night school in New York to learn English, he was an advocate of formal education. He made sure that his children went to school to continue on his path of attaining the American Dream. Although he spoke to his children in the Neapolitan dialect, he also conversed with them in English. When my parents spoke to me and my brother, they always spoke in English. When they and Nonno did not want us to know what they were saying, they spoke in the Neapolitan dialect.

Nonno also spoke the "real" Italian--Dante's Italian. When I was in high school, he helped me develop my Italian writing, listening, reading, and speaking skills. In the evenings, after I finished my homework and he finished reading the newspaper, he would listen to me read aloud from my favorite textbook, *Le Avventure di Giovanni Passaguai* (*The Adventures of Hard Luck Johnny*), by Aristide Masella. As I read the stories aloud in Italian, we would laugh at the trouble Giovanni got himself into as he tried to do a good deed. Each story was followed by comprehension questions, completion items, and multiple-choice items. I would write the answers and read them to Nonno who would correct me if I made any errors.

In 1968, my junior year in high school, I was selected to represent my Italian class in a New York City-wide contest sponsored by the American Association of Teachers of Italian. To prepare for the competition, Nonno coached me as I memorized and practiced reciting "X Agosto" by Giovanni Pascoli. My family was very proud when I won a copy of Michael Angelo Musmanno's book, *The Story of the Italians in America*. I am embarrassed to admit that it wasn't until I became interested in my family roots, more than 40 years after receiving it, that I finally read it.

With Nonno's continued support, I was able to complete four years of Italian in three, and I think he was proud of me when I was awarded a scholarship from the Columbia Association of the Board of Education, and I received the Italian medal at my high school graduation. Nonno's interest and attention contributed to my success in the study of Italian. After more than fifty years, I am trying to re-learn Italian. I wish Nonno were still here to help me.

Joy and Tears of Happiness

I believe that a highlight for Nonno was attending his oldest grandson Richard's graduation from St. Francis College in Brooklyn. The graduation was on Wednesday, June 6, 1970, at the Brooklyn Academy of Music. When Richard's name was announced as first in his class, graduating *summa cum laude* with a Bachelor of Science degree in biology, Nonno stood up and with tears in his eyes he proudly exclaimed, "That's my grandson!" Richard observed that Nonno was more excited than he was. Unfortunately, Nonno did not live to see Richard achieve more accolades, becoming a distinguished dentist and chief of dentistry at the VA Hospital in Albany, New York.

As all doting grandfathers, I observed that Nonno was extremely happy when he witnessed his family growing. His second oldest grandson, Henry Jr., was his first grandchild to marry. The wedding was on Saturday, September 1, 1973. Nonno was so distracted by all the excitement that he inadvertently neglected to put his medicated inhaler in his pocket. While traveling from Staten Island to the ceremony and the reception in New Jersey, Nonno realized that he didn't have his inhaler and he started to panic. My father, who was driving the car, managed to find a pharmacy that was open on a Saturday afternoon (without any cell phone or global positioning system devices in those days), to get the inhaler that Nonno needed. He immediately applied the medication and felt relieved and calm, enabling him to enjoy the ceremony and the outdoor festivities.

Gardening

Nonno had a "green thumb." I notice from photos that in the front of his house he had a *giardino*, a flower garden with a variety of seasonal plants—roses, philodendra, and hydrangea. He loved the garden—planting seeds, bushes, trees. He also tended to an *orto*, a vegetable garden—growing *pomodori* (tomatoes), *zucchini* (squash), and *fagiolini* (stringbeans), During the spring and summer he was always outside enjoying the warm weather, watering the plants and the lawn. He had such a reputation for cultivating a garden that the neighbors would ask him for his advice and help (see photo). He was always willing to assist. The only complaint I remember him having was getting bug bites, but it never stopped him from tending the plants. He said his "medals" for all of his work were the bug bites.

Frances R. Curcio

Nonno helping Lena, a neighbor, planting flowers.
— Cipolaro/Curcio Family Album

    A big project that he was always involved in was planting and canning *pomodori*. Nonno assisted my parents in this extensive amount of work. Many times, they purchased additional bushels of pomodori. They washed the pomodori, cut them, and cooked them in huge pots that looked like cauldrons. While the pomodori were cooking, Nonno helped to sterilize the jars in which the pomodori would be stored. Throughout the year, my mother would use the jars of pomodori in various recipes, especially making pasta with gravy. We all reaped the benefits of this extraordinary amount of work. As Nonno and my parents aged, this became too much work for them, and I was involved in other activities, unable to volunteer to take over.

Being a Responsible Citizen

    Nonno cherished the privilege of becoming an American citizen. Every November he practiced his civic duty by exercising his right to vote. Before I was able to drive and to vote, Nonno and my parents drove to the polling place together. Once I had my driver's license, I was their "chauffeur," and we all went to vote together.

Nonno had to relinquish his Italian citizenship to become an American citizen. When the United States officially entered World War I on April 6, 1917, about three years after the war had started, Nonno had already applied for U. S. citizenship. He filed his "Intent to Naturalize" papers on April 18, 1917, and he also dutifully registered with the armed forces to serve in the War. Since he was married with children, he was exempt from conscription.

Nonno understood that American citizenship was a trust he had to hold as sacred. Knowing his character and personality, I am sure that during the five years he waited to become an American citizen, he fulfilled the requirements described by John J. D. Trenor:

It is the duty further of every applicant for citizenship to exalt the standard of American citizenship in his personal conduct and by every influence at his command. He should be sober, truthful, honest, law-abiding, industrious, thrifty and ambitious for the advance of himself and his children. He should prize the free thought, free press, free school and free government of America as a treasure beyond price. He should learn to rely with confidence on American laws, juries and judges for justice and indemnity for wrongs and not to seek redress by lawless violence. He should never forget that prejudice can most surely be confounded by conduct that may defy the barbs of slander, and that any falling off from this standard of duty will lower not only himself but the reputation of his fellow countrymen in the esteem of America. Let it be his pride to keep ever at heart 'I was an Italian. I am an American. 1 am not conscious that I have done anything to sully the honor of either name.'[14]

14. Lord, Trenor, and Barrows, *The Italian in America*, p. 256-257.

Once he became an American citizen in 1922, he proudly flew the American flag on his property (see photo below). His devotion to his adoptive country served as a role model for his sons when it was their turn to serve their country. When they were of age at the onset of WW II, they enlisted in the Army, and they were honored to serve from 1941 to 1945. Amedeo served as a technical sergeant and administrative specialist. He was stationed at Mitchel Field, Uniondale, Long Island, New York. Henry was a First Sergeant in the Army Air Corps and was awarded the prestigious Legion of Merit for his heroic service in the North African Theater of Operations. Nonno must have had conflicting feelings with his sons fighting for America against Italy. Perhaps he was relieved when Italy joined the allied powers on October 13, 1943. Nonno was proud to pose with his sons in their uniforms (see photo of Nonno with Amedeo and Henry).

1101 Tompkins Avenue, Staten Island;
Nonno's house where he proudly flew the American flag.
— Cipolaro/Curcio Family Album

Nonno proudly posing with his sons, Henry and Amedeo.
— Cipolaro/Curcio Family Album

Helping in the Ocean Sweet Shoppe

In 1964, Uncle Amedeo purchased a candy store—the Ocean Sweet Shoppe, on Ocean Avenue, in South Beach. For about ten years, my mother would drive Nonno to the store, where she served customers from behind the counter and he helped by organizing the comic books, the pretzels, and the candy racks. I often observed him animatedly chatting with customers. He also watched out for shoplifters, although everyone seemed to be honest in those days. As he would say in the Neapolitan dialect, "*passatiempu.*" He would look forward to passing some time, about four hours a day, Monday through Friday, in the candy store.

Nonno Totore at the Ocean Sweet Shoppe counter; circa 1967.
— Courtesy of John K. Cipolaro.

Towards the End

Nonno had just turned 83 years old when in March 1973, his sister-in-law, Mary, my great aunt, passed away. My family and I went to the funeral home and to the burial. One afternoon at the funeral parlor, I sat behind Nonno who was speaking with his brother, Zio Livio, and I heard him say, *"È vicino"*—It's near. I was troubled by this. Was Nonno not feeling well? Had he been to see the doctor and not mentioned it to anyone? Was he predicting his demise? I never asked.

After the funeral, life went on…We celebrated my graduation from college. Just as he did in 1970 for Richard's graduation, Nonno came to the Brooklyn Academy of Music on Saturday, June 9, and witnessed the conferral of my Bachelor of Science degree in mathematics, *cum laude*, from St. Francis College. After the ceremony he hugged and kissed me as tears of joy streamed down his face. I, too, was emotional and I felt blessed to have him witness my accomplishment.

As I was completing my exams and preparing for graduation, my brother and I were planning a surprise party for our parents' twenty-fifth wedding anniversary. We decided not to tell Nonno because we were worried that he might innocently slip and reveal the secret. When the day came, I told him so he could get ready. I felt terrible keeping the secret from him, and to this day, I am not sure whether he was hurt not knowing the secret sooner. I hope not.

For many years I never thought about life without Nonno. It was only after he died that I realized what a profound impact he had on me as I was growing up. When he died, he took a part of me and all of us with him. But there is still a special place in my heart for him and for all my memories. Years after he died, I did not know that I would have so many questions. In particular, I wondered what his life was like as a child in Contursi-Terme. I have attempted to answer my questions by reading about life in Contursi and visiting the commune as often as possible.

Frances R. Curcio

Bisnonni Margherita and Alfonso Cipollaro; circa 1900.
— Cipolaro/Sorrentino Family Album; Courtesy of Rosanne Denaro.

Life in Contursi-Terme

"My long lost land was one that,
when snows enveloped it, did not erase a sun that
still in my dream was lit..."
— JOSEPH TUSIANI[15]

As a young child, Nonno developed a love of family, friends, and his familiar surroundings. I am sure that he cherished all of these in his heart, but I must begin his story with his father, Alfonso.

I believe that my *Bisnonno*, my great-grandfather, was a forward-looking man. Born on June 9, 1845, during the period of the *Risorgimento* (1815-1870), the time when Italy achieved national unity and independence, Alfonso was *un sarto*, a tailor. A respectable member of the commune, Bisnonno *un artigiano*, an artisan/craftsman, was a landowner and a homeowner. On March 20, 1871, Alfonso married Margherita Santalucia, a Contursian who was born on October 14, 1852 (see photo of Alfonso and Margherita). Their wedding, their baptisms, and the baptisms of their ten children took place in Chiesa S.S. Maria degli Angeli, the commune's ninth-century basilica (see photos of the altar and baptismal font).

Bisnonno's two-story house provided living quarters on the upper level, and a place for animals on the lower level. He also had a tailor shop next to his house where he worked and prepared two of his sons to become tailors.

---

15. Tusiani, *Gente Mia*, p. 6.

Frances R. Curcio

Baptismal Font, Chiesa Santa Maria degli Angeli, dated 1582, Contursi.
— *Curcio Family Album.*

Main altar of Chiesa Santa Maria degli Angeli, Contursi-Terme.
— *Curcio Family Album.*

Based on documents in the *Municipio*, Bisnonno was active in the political life of the commune, attending town meetings, serving on committees, and successfully refuting an attempt on the part of the local Catholic church to appropriate some of his land. Although there was animosity and skepticism toward the church because the clergy took advantage of *contadini*, the peasants' ignorance, and tried to instill the fear of God in them to comply, the *artigiani* tried to curry favor with priests by attending mass and making generous contributions to the church. On the one hand, when it came to attending mass regularly, the men in Southern Italy were not as devout as the women. On the other hand, with at least nine religious sites for worship established throughout the years in the small Contursi commune with an estimated population of only a few thousand in the late 1880s, it suggests that the Contursians were very religious people. They constructed and supported six churches (S. Maria degli Angeli, S. Donato, Bambino, Carmine, S. Maria della Scalella, S. Vito); two chapels (S. Antonio, Madonnella); and one sanctuary (Madonna delle Grazie).

Alfonso and Margherita had ten children together—five boys and five girls (see the family tree, page 92). For the majority of children in Southern Italy, formal schooling for boys was typically not common and not encouraged by fathers who did not trust government institutions. However, Bisnonno Alfonso was supportive of his sons improving their chances for a productive, prosperous future. According to the manifest of the steamship that transported Nonno to *l'America*, he was able to read and write upon entry at Ellis Island.

Life in Southern Italy was not literately rich. In the communes, there were rarely books and newspapers in the homes. However, books about the saints were found in many homes of the *artigiani*. Most likely, Bisnonno Alfonso had access to such books and periodically obtained and read a newspaper.

Early Education and Childhood

I can only imagine what school was like for the boys in Contursi. They spoke a version of the Neapolitan dialect at home, but they had to learn the language of Dante to be able to read and write in the "official" Italian language.[16] According to the Italian 1877 Coppino law, the boys went to school free of charge for three years, between the ages of six and nine.[17] For the most part, the law was not enforced in the *Mezzogiorno*, in Southern Italy, but Bisnonno Alfonso had his sons take advantage of the opportunity. In 1904, the year that Nonno left for America, compulsory education was extended to the age of twelve.[18]

According to Leonard Covello, the teachers were very strict, severe, didactic, poorly prepared, and very poorly paid, with male teachers rarely earning more than 750 lira per year (i.e., about $150 at the time), slightly more per year than female teachers.[19] The one book that Nonno's older brother Livio used was most likely also used by Nonno when it was his turn to go to school. Typically, the book was bulky, poorly printed, and it had very few, if any, pictures.[20] The lessons consisted of Italian composition, oral dictation, mental arithmetic, reading, and history, geography, and citizenship,[21] all to various degrees of depth. The instructional content was all in one book. Learning was by rote, recitation, and repetition—building one's memory. Due to the lack of government funds, which were controlled by Northern Italy, and the lack of attention to supporting education in the south, the buildings that housed schools in Southern Italy were noted as being inadequate, overcrowded, and unsanitary.[22] Historically, autocratic powers did not support education for the lower classes so as to suppress them by

---

16. The language used in formal settings much before the unification of Italy, and not officially included in the Constitution until 2007 (https://italyexplained.com/blame-dante-how-a-dialect-became-a-language/).

17. Williams, *South Italian Folkways.*

18. Covello, *Social Background of the Italo-American School Child.*

19. *Ibid.*

20. *Ibid.*

21. Williams, *South Italian Folkways.*

22. Villari, *Italian Life in Town and Country.*

Mio Nonno Totore and The American Dream

keeping them ignorant and subservient. The Church was also notorious for keeping the southern Italians in intellectual bondage by not supporting educational programs for all children. Although they spent a minimal amount of time in school, it was fortunate for Nonno and his brothers to have a father who realized the potential of being formally educated.

Childhood for Nonno was not at all like childhood in America as we know of it today. In 19th century Italy and many other countries throughout the world at the time, children were viewed as miniature adults, and they were strictly disciplined. Play time was minimal to nonexistent. In addition to attending school, as early as age 5 or 6, the boys were apprenticed to learn a trade. They were getting *un'educazione*, that is, moral and practical training.[23] Alfonso, *un sarto*, taught Livio and Nonno Salvatore the art of Neapolitan tailoring, and as future custom tailors, they mastered the use of the metric tape measure. School in the town was in session from September first to the middle of June, whereas school in the country had a different schedule based on planting and harvesting. School was held daily including Saturday, typically from 8 AM to 12 PM, and then following the afternoon recess for lunch and rest, 2 PM to 4 PM.

While the boys went to school or practiced their tailoring skills, their sisters helped their mother, Margherita, *una tessitrice*, a weaver, and they learned how to sew and cook. Husbands were found for four of the girls, Cristina, Luigia, Battilda, and Marieta. At the time, it was taboo to marry outside the immediate community, so Alfonso most likely had arranged the betrothals. One sister, Florinda, remained single. A talented seamstress, she offered sewing lessons to the girls and women in the commune.

Similarly, Alfonso was also most likely involved in selecting spouses for his sons. Living down a small path from Piazza Garibaldi was Antoinetta, the daughter of Filomena who was Alfonso's

---

23. Covello, *Social Background of the Italo-American School Child.*

first cousin. Nonno Totore and Antoinetta were second cousins. Antoinetta's husband Enrico Vece was a builder, also considered an *artigiano*. Enrico and Antoinetta's eldest child, a daughter, Ettora, two years younger than Nonno, was his second cousin once removed. It is highly likely that the two fathers expected to strengthen their ties through the marriage of Totore and Ettora. During their brief time in Contursi, Nonno and Ettora were childhood acquaintances. Almost ten years after arriving in America, fulfilling a familial promise, Totore married Ettora.

Children in Contursi and the other small communes developed a sense of responsibility and duty to the family from a very young age. Living in the small commune of Contursi cultivated common values, beliefs, mores, and instilled the development of a strong work ethic. Nonno's family lived in the center of the commune, and their house was on the perimeter of Piazza Garibaldi, the main square across from the *Municipio*. Not too far from their house were the therapeutic, thermal hot and cold springs, that attracted health-conscious visitors, and hence the term "Terme" in the name of the commune: Contursi-Terme. The medicinal benefits are attributed to the different sulfurous, lithia, and alkaline waters. The early Romans recognized the suitability of the springs for their baths. Much before Contursi was established as a commune in 1582, such ancient philosophers as Aristotle (384-322 BCE), Virgil (71-20 BCE), and Pliny (23/24-79 CE), alluded to the natural, rich resources in the area in their writings.[24]

As she aged, one of Nonno's older sisters, Florinda, developed health problems and taking advantage of the location, her physician, Dr. Feruccio Forlenza,[25] prescribed thermal bath treatment. It may have provided temporary relief, but she progressively worsened and in 1957, she passed away while visiting her older sister Cristina and her family in Lioni. She was buried in the Carfagna family mausoleum in Lioni.

---

24. Borzellino, *Contursi Terme.*

25. The Cipollaro, Forelenza, and the Vece families were related.

Mio Nonno Totore and The American Dream

Saints' Days and Holidays

Typical of most families in Southern Italy, saints' feast days were the main forms of recreation for Nonno and his family. During these special feasts and festivals, itinerant minstrels and entertainers conversant in multiple dialects, visited and entertained in the various communes during the festivities and during *Carnevale* (i.e., Carnival week before the beginning of the Lenten season). The entertainers practiced the arts of puppetry and *contastorie*, public storytelling, and they offered puppet theater performances. The subjects of the shows were based on operas, musical theater, and plays about the saints and Christian heroes. The local priests determined the suitability and decency of the acts and performances for children and adults. Families that could not offer a fee in currency for performances, contributed in-kind with food (e.g., *verdure*, vegetables; *frutta*, fruits from their *orti*, gardens) dropped into a *piattino*, a collection bowl. A part of cultural tradition and entertainment for the poor, puppet performances were modeled after the marionettes that were created and developed in Sicily and in Venice. *Teatro dei pupi*, puppet theaters, became so popular among children that the Church adopted the venue for religious education. As a small child, Nonno most likely sat and watched with wonder as the puppets were "brought to life" to reveal the moral of their stories.

One of the special festivals that has always been celebrated on August 7th, is the Feast of San Donato, patron saint of Contursi, noted for curing afflictions and deformities of the body, including fits, and paralysis. Everyone in the commune took a break from work and school to pay homage to the saint. A statue and images of the saint were on display. In many communes the men carried saints' statues, parading through the streets and piazzas (see photo). This tradition carried over into the Little Italys in the United States, where money is pinned onto the clothes of the statue of the celebrated saints. In the early to middle parts of the twentieth century, the feast of San Donato was celebrated in Tompkinsville, Staten Island, a center of immigrants from Contursi. It was called "Little Contursi." I remember as a

41

Statue of San Donato being paraded through the streets in Contursi-Terme.
— Courtesy of Giovanni D'Angelo

Mio Nonno Totore and The American Dream

child attending the feast on Monroe Avenue. Strings of lights were po-
sitioned on wires overhead. I recall plenty of food, games, and happy
people. My Uncle Amedeo, Nonno's older son, and his family lived on
Monroe Avenue. We visited them every week, but this feast was special. It was outdoors and there were many people from the neighborhood whom Nonno knew from his younger years. He always seemed
to be very content to be among them. This feast gave Nonno a chance
to reconnect with his fellow Contursians.

Simple Meals

Before going to school or to work in his father's tailor shop,
Nonno had *colazione* (breakfast) consisting of *pane*, bread; *formaggio*,
cheese; and perhaps some *verdure,* vegetables from the *orto*, tended to
by his sisters. Sometime around mid-day, the men and boys would take
a break for their *pranzo*, their main meal of the day consisting of *polenta*
made with corn meal, *minestra*-soup made with escarole and beans, or
maccheroni with *cibo di polso*, pulse food including dry peas, chickpeas,
beans, lentils; or *patate,* potatoes; *formaggio, insalata*; salad with *sedano*,
celery; *rapanelli*, radishes; *pane*; and *frutta*. There was very little, if any,
carne, meat, served except perhaps on special holidays. The main meal
was followed by a siesta, before resuming work or school. In the evening before retiring to sleep, everyone ate a very light meal, the *cena*,
consisting of food similar to *pranzo* but less substantial. Meals were
accompanied by homemade wine. In Contursi as in the other southern
communes, there was very little *zucchero*, sugar. *Biscotti*, biscuits; *mar-
mellata*, jam; and *burro*, butter were not part of the daily diet. I think
having these culinary experiences taught Nonno to eat in moderation,
especially while being around a crowded table with his family consisting of twelve people. Was there enough food for everyone? Did they
usually leave the table satisfied or hungry?

The town of Contursi-Terme, Italy.

Leaving Contursi-Terme

"But I know what it's like to leave your home and country behind, and to start anew. And I can say that the departure, however final it seems, is never forever. You carry both within you, always. They are a constant presence, sometimes near, sometimes far, lighting up the path to the future."
— ZANNA SLONIOWSKA[26]

In 1884, the year Nonno's oldest brother Livio was born, and six years before Nonno was born, Southern Italy was plagued with malaria and cholera. Other diseases that were threatening the population were trachoma, a highly contagious bacterial infection affecting the eyes caused by unsanitary conditions, and tuberculosis, a serious bacterial infection affecting the lungs. During the late 1880s into the early 1890s, the health conditions in Southern Italy worsened. Although the causes of death were not recorded, two of Nonno's older brothers, Amedeo and Giuseppe, were young when they died. Furthermore, when Nonno was born in 1890, the economy in Italy at the time and during his early childhood years was gravely depressive with the value of the lira extremely weak. Was Bisnonno aware and disappointed with the great differences between government support and funding in Northern Italy and Southern Italy, with Southern Italy in greater need, receiving the short end of the stick? From the 1870s

---

26. Sloniowska, "I Left Ukraine 20 Years Ago," p. A21.

onward, life in Southern Italy was *una miseria*, a misery.[27] Most likely all these factors gave Bisnonno Alfonso pause, and he became interested in sending his sons to *L'America*. But how did Alfonso learn about the opportunities and challenges that existed across the ocean? Did he realize that the journey from Naples, Italy, to New York City, would be 7,095 kilometers (i.e., 4,409 miles) across the vast Atlantic Ocean and that it could take between 12 and 15 days by steamship? If he had heard about the "gold rush" in *L'America*, did he believe that the streets were paved with *oro*, gold? Could he have heard how immigrants of various nationalities, especially Italians, were being exploited? Perhaps some of his Contursian acquaintances left and returned to share their experiences. Perhaps he heard that the Italian government was encouraging people to emigrate, offering free passports to those who leave. Perhaps he read about opportunities in the New World. I have many questions, but no answers...

In 1901, the first year that the Italian government offered free passports, Livio was 17 years old. Although at the time, the United States government did not require passports for those entering through Ellis Island, emigrants sailing from Italy were required to have a passport,[28] so Livio had to apply for a free passport in the provincial office in Salerno. As Alfonso's oldest son, he was the first to be sent to the United States, leaving from Naples aboard the *Nord America*. Most likely, before leaving Contursi for *L'America*, Livio visited his oldest sister Cristina and her family in Lioni. After he said his goodbyes and embraced his mother and his siblings, I expect that Alfonso went with him to Naples to watch him board the steamship. According to the ship manifest, is not clear whether he had a sponsor. Livio arrived at Ellis Island on June 15th. It was recorded that he was to live on East Houston Street in Manhattan, but it was family knowledge that he spent some

---

27. Banfield, *The Moral Basis of a Backward Society.*

28. Foerster, *The Italian Emigration of Our Times.* Passports were required in the U.S. for everyone starting in 1907.

of his time at 66 Mulberry Street. After getting settled in a small room shared with other Italian immigrants, most likely, he wrote to his father to announce his arrival in New York. He corresponded with his father regularly, and when he had money, he respectfully and dutifully sent money home.

As a personable young man, I believe that Livio maintained connections with Contursians who were arriving and returning, managing to keep his father informed, encouraging him to send Totore to New York. Not wanting to alarm his father or discourage him from sending Totore, I think that Livio chose not to report about the horrific conditions that he had to endure while in steerage aboard the steamship. He also did not describe the deplorable conditions of the tenement building where he was living in Little Italy. Early in the year in 1904, I believe that Livio must have written to tell his father that a Contursian, Nunziante Forlenza, living at 23 Mulberry Street, down the block from Livio, would be sponsoring his uncle, Antonio, and his 17-year-old cousin, Temistocle. I believe that Livio convinced his father to send Totore with Antonio and Temistocle.[29] I expect that Livio sent some money to his father to help pay for the 15,000 lire steamship ticket in steerage for Totore (about US$30, at the time, about $1010 in 2023 dollars). Twenty-year-old Livio was Totore's sponsor and his name and address at 66 Mulberry Street, appeared on the ship manifest.

By 1904, Southern Italy was characterized by physical, social, intellectual, and regional turmoil. The living conditions in Italy and the encouragement from Livio convinced Alfonso to send Totore to the United States. Knowing Antonio and Temistocle, who was a tailor, he decided to take Livio's advice and send his fourteen-year-old son along with them, asking Antonio to watch out for young Totore. The time was right to send Nonno to the New World.

---

29. According to genealogical records, Antonio and Temistocle may have been distant relatives of Bisnonno Alfonso, whose Zia Gaetana was married to Alfonso Forlenza. In the small Contursi commune, everyone must have been related in some way and to some degree.

Although a passport was not required for those entering the U. S. through Ellis Island in 1904, it is highly likely that Totore did have one. Even if the decision to send Totore to be with Livio may have happened quickly, I am sure that Alfonso took Totore to the provincial office in Salerno to apply for a passport.

On the morning that Totore was scheduled to leave Contursi, I imagine that he neatly put the few hand-me-down clothes that he had in a cloth satchel made by his mother, and he slipped into his one pair of shoes. Overcome with sadness that Totore was leaving, her tears must have fallen onto the *pane, formaggio, peperoni,* and *pomodori* that she packed for him. Since Livio sent money to his father, I believe that Alfonso gave Totore some U. S. dollars. From his experience, Livio must have explained that immigrants were expected to have some U.S. money upon arrival to enter *L'America*.

I can imagine a tearful farewell at the Contursi train station. Before boarding the train to Naples, Nonno must have embraced his mother and father, not knowing that he would never see them again. I expect that there were seven siblings at the station to bid farewell— Luigia, Florinda, Battilda, Amedeo, Giuseppe, Tullio, and Marieta. His oldest sister, Cristina, was in Lioni with her husband, Pasquale Carfagna, and their three children, four-year-old Gennaro, three-year-old Margherita, and one-year-old Amedeo. Nonno must have visited them several days before his departure. More than fifty years would pass before he would see Cristina again with her adult children and grandchildren.

Livio was anticipating Totore's arrival in New York. I can only speculate what Nonno was thinking and feeling. On the one hand, I often wonder whether he wanted to leave. Did he tearfully plead with his mother to ask his father to let him stay? However, on the other hand, it is possible that Nonno may have been enthusiastic about joining Livio in America and he may have begged his father to send him. He would be embarking on an adventure. But, in either case, I think about my comfortable life at fourteen years of age, and I realize how heart-wrenching and unsettling it must have been for him to be torn away from everything familiar. At his age, he probably neither understood nor appreciated that sending him away was an act of love and hope for a better future.

Antonio and Temistocle's family was also at the train station, saying *arrivederci*. Nonno boarded the train with them en route to Naples. He had his first experience of functioning outside his "comfort zone." I wonder whether Nonno looked back as he boarded the train.

Based on accounts by immigrants who documented their ordeal, it is possible that when they deboarded the train, they walked about 10 minutes to the pier where they checked in, received their ship cards, and boarded a small boat to get vaccinated by the ship's physician. The vaccination was required due to an outbreak of smallpox in the United States.[30] After being inoculated, they must have returned to the pier to find a place to stay while waiting to embark on the steamship *Sardegna*, which arrived from Genoa after initially boarding passengers from the northern regions. Like thousands of other Italians, Nonno and his companions traveled in steerage.

Steamship Sardegna; circa 1900.

---

30. Reported in *The New York Times* in January and May 1904.

The steamship *Sardegna,* was built in 1901, by Bacini of Riva Trigoso in Northern Italy, for general navigation between Italy and New York. Its capacity was 1,449 passengers of whom 80 were first class, 45 were second class, and 1,324 were third class, or steerage. Nonno was one of the 1,000+ passengers in steerage. Although it may seem as though there were limits placed on the number of passengers, it is highly likely that more passengers were added to steerage than the number that could be accommodated. Overcrowding was not unusual. After arriving from Genoa and boarding passengers in Naples, the steamship left on Friday, 3 June 1904, for the thirteen-day voyage to Ellis Island.

Life in Steerage

"When the ship rocked and over the thumping
of engines the babies were crying and men
and women crying to God for mercy
I tried to imagine America--Liberty
like a tower, her torch..."
— BERT STERN[31]

After boarding the steamship and submitting their ship cards, Nonno and his companions were assigned to a large compartment in steerage, literally and figuratively, in the bowels of the boat. A space originally designed to store equipment and located below the waterline next to the steering equipment, steerage housed more than one thousand passengers, organized in compartments. Nonno's compartment accommodated about 300 men. Other compartments in different parts of steerage were for families and for women traveling alone. Antonio and the boys were directed to follow a crowd of men below deck. With the advent of great numbers of passengers seeking passage to the New World, the area was designated for hordes of people. Unlike the accommodations for first- and second-class passengers who traveled in comfort in the privacy of their own cabins, Nonno and his companions were assigned to their own berths. According to Dillingham's 1911 document, *The Reports of the Immigration Commission*, the berths were 6 feet long and 2 feet wide. Small and lean, most likely, Nonno took a top berth.

---

31. Stern, "Steerage," p. 137.

The steerage passengers had barely enough room for themselves, and they had to keep their traveling bags with them in their berths. There were 2 feet and 6 inches of space above each berth. They had to be careful not to get up too quickly to avoid banging their heads. The berth was made of iron with a straw-filled mattress, a blanket, and a life preserver to serve as a pillow. During the voyage, the berths were never serviced or cleaned by the stewards. (I wonder whether they were cleaned before the next group of passengers arrived.) "The sleeping quarters were always dismal, damp, dirty, and [a] most unwholesome place. The air was heavy, foul, and deadening to the spirit and the mind."[32]

Furthermore, there were no "sick cans," or waste baskets provided. Conditions were spartan and the sanitary conditions were abysmal. To avoid the smell of excrement, urine, and vomit, I am sure that Nonno retreated as often as possible to the open deck areas whenever the weather was conducive, but unfortunately, the outdoor space was limited so most likely it was very crowded. For thirteen days they had to endure inadequate heating and ventilation whenever they were in their sleeping spaces.[33] To keep warm, I imagine that Nonno always had to remain fully dressed, sleeping in his clothes. Was he able to sleep or get any rest while ill passengers were moaning and suffering from seasickness? Was he a victim of seasickness? Although there were medical facilities on the steamship, they were not for treating seasickness. There were other illnesses that were contracted in such close quarters: cholera, yellow fever, smallpox, dysentery. Nonno was very lucky not to succumb to these illnesses and he was among the one in ten who survived the journey without any serious health problems.

Typically, there were two small washrooms available for the steerage passengers. Cold salt water was available from most of the faucets, with warm water provided from only one faucet. Soap and towels were not provided. The multi-purpose basins were used as a dishpan to wash greasy tin plates and laundry, and to serve as a receptable for vomit. The

---

32. Dillingham, *The Reports of the Immigration Commission*, p. 35.

33. *Ibid.*

Mio Nonno Totore and The American Dream

basins were not regularly cleaned.[34] Given the lack of facilities and inattention to maintain cleanliness, I imagine that it was virtually impossible for Nonno and his companions to maintain their personal hygiene.

It is no surprise that for all the years after arriving in New York, Livio and Nonno never talked about their experiences in steerage.[35] It was obviously a time in their lives they wanted to forget. To address inadequate inhumane conditions in steerage, international laws were imposed to improve conditions by 1904, but inspections by the Immigration Commission did not report much improvement. Nonno was subjected to and endured truly horrific conditions that cannot be adequately described in words.

"Dining" in Steerage

"Dining" is definitely not the word to describe the process of eating in steerage. Nonno and the other passengers had "food tickets" to obtain large pans for their food. They had to wash and care for their dishes and utensils. If the weather permitted, they ate their food on the open deck. In bad weather, there were no other options but to eat in their sleeping berth.

Coffee grounds mixed with sugar, milk, and warm water were offered for beverage. It has been reported that the meat and fish that were served were old and foul smelling. The vegetables were unrecognizable, and the butter was inedible. Some of the meals may have been better than others, but they were few and far between. Passengers who had money were able to purchase fruit, candy, and alcoholic beverages. It is a wonder that Nonno survived for thirteen days on such a non-nutritious diet.

Although required daily, medical inspection was typically performed only once after sailing, and just before arrival, but the passengers' health cards were punched multiple times, faking inspections. The

---

34. *Ibid.*

35. According to LaGumina (1979), this was typical of most Italian immigrants.

day before arriving at Ellis Island, the ship cards that were originally collected upon embarkation and health cards were returned to the passengers to present to the physicians at Ellis Island. What a travesty!

Occupying leisure time was left up to each passenger. Some small spaces in steerage may have been available for walking, dancing, playing games (e.g., *Scopa* and *Briscola*), and exercising.

Many of the requirements stipulated in the United States Passenger Act of 1882 were not consistently followed for all vessels transporting immigrants to America. Captains of the vessels were to be held accountable for inadequacies, but inspections rarely occurred and very few captains were ever disciplined.

As the long arduous journey was almost over, prior to entering New York harbor, the steamship dropped anchor in the Lower Bay to fulfill quarantine requirements. I am sure that Nonno and most of his fellow emigrants wondered why the ship had stopped. He may have excitedly scrambled onto the deck to see whether they had arrived, and he may have seen the shores of "the Promised Land," which were actually Brooklyn and Staten Island. He may have noticed U. S. inspectors boarding the steamship, but he may not have been aware that the inspectors had to review the manifest records and health status of the passengers. How much time was required for this review? Several hours? Historical weather records indicate that it would have been pleasant for Nonno to stay on deck during the review. Once the review was completed, the captain was permitted to lift anchor and proceed to the Hudson River, where the steamship was to dock. The inspectors remained on the steamship until docking.

Approaching the Statue of Liberty

"Give me your tired, your poor,
Your huddled masses yearning to breathe free,
The wretched refuse of your teeming shore.
Send these, the homeless, tempest-tost to me,
I lift my lamp beside the golden door!"
— EMMA LAZARUS[36]

It was as though summer had already arrived on Thursday, 16 June, 1904. Without any rain in the forecast, the sun danced on the water with the temperature recorded at 80 degrees inland. With the light breeze from the water, it was a little bit cooler. After being in quarantine and given permission to proceed by the U. S. inspectors, as the steamship *Sardegna* began its approach into the Upper Bay of New York Harbor, I am sure that the passengers excitedly clamored to the open decks. After thirteen very long days at sea, everyone was indeed tired, physically and mentally exhausted, and eager to experience the first sight of land. The ship sailed through the calm waters of the Narrows.

Nonno's heart must have been racing and his adrenaline flowing as he and his companions were joined by others who rushed up to the deck. Perhaps they had to wedge their way through the hordes of people to position themselves close to the rails to witness the gradual appearance of the Statue of Liberty—*La Statua* sculpted by the French artist Frédéric Auguste Bartholdi—which had been welcoming immigrants

---

36. Eiselein, *Emma Lazarus*, p. 20.

Immigrants on a ship approaching the Statue of Liberty and Ellis Island.
— Photo in the Public Domain

Mio Nonno Totore and The American Dream

since 1886. As the ship progressed, the majestic 19th -century statue, also known as "Liberty Enlightening the World," seemed to grow in size, welcoming and thrilling Nonno and all the other passengers. I wonder what Nonno was thinking. Did he move thoughts about Contursi to the back of his mind to focus on this experience as an adventure? Was he upset with his father for sending him away? Was he thinking about finally seeing his brother Livio after three years that they were apart?

The enormous statue may have captured his attention and distracted him from all of his thoughts. Many of the Catholic immigrants equated the statue with the Madonna, praying to her for the promise of a better life in the new land. The poor, wretched folks in steerage, most of whom were illiterate, were not familiar with the welcoming text on the bronze plaque, "The New Colossus," by Emma Lazarus, installed in 1903, the year before Nonno arrived. Most likely it wasn't until Nonno studied for his naturalization exam many years after his arrival, that he understood fully the meaning of the statue and life in America.

Ellis Island.

Arriving at Ellis Island

"by ellis island i mean existing in two worlds
at the same time
some pieces break off in one world and go
on living there
other fragments move on to a next world and
there flourish…"
— ROBERT VISCUSI[37]

Once the steamship docked, first- and second-class passengers were inspected at the pier, and then released. Nonno and the other steerage passengers were given cards with their manifest numbers on them. Nonno's number was 9. Disembarkation from the ship was organized by number. Steerage passengers boarded a ferry to take them to Ellis Island for health checks conducted by the United States Public Health Service doctors. There were lines of passengers waiting to check in, showing their documents, and preparing for the health check. I can imagine that this must have been anxiety-provoking and stressful for everyone, not knowing whether they would pass inspection and worried that they might be sent back to Italy. Did Nonno know what to expect? Perhaps emigrants who returned to Italy had shared their experiences with Nonno before he left. Was he torn between staying in the New World and wanting to return to his home in Contursi? Was he worried about disappointing his brother Livio, who invested

---

37. Viscusi, *ellis island*, p. 221.

time and money in his voyage? Being the optimistic, positive person I knew him to be, I am sure Nonno convinced himself that everything would be fine.

As the passengers disembarked the ferry, they entered the Great Hall. They were instructed to leave their luggage, satchels, and bags on the first floor. While they entered and dropped off their belongings, medics observed the immigrants' behaviors from the second-floor balcony: Did they notice people who had difficulty breathing? Were there people who had difficulty walking? They looked out for any who manifested aberrant behaviors.

When Nonno reached the second floor, he was examined for trachoma by a medic who used a buttonhole hook, flipping up his eyelids. This standard practice must have been painful. It was reported that some people had adverse reactions to the procedure, temporarily affecting their vision. I wonder whether Nonno had a vision problem. I remember that he always wore glasses. After waiting for his turn to be examined, the medic spent approximately two minutes

Inspectors checking for trachoma; Ellis Island; circa 1900.
— Photo in the public domain.

Mio Nonno Totore and The American Dream

Buttonhole hooks used to flip back eyelids to check for trachoma.
— Photo from display on Ellis Island.

examining Nonno's hair, scalp, and his body. I believe being a young adolescent was in his favor. He was strong and healthy, so the medics did not refer him for further analysis. He was ready to meet his brother Livio and start his new life, but he was placed in "detention" until Livio arrived to "claim" him. According to the official records, Nonno was dismissed in Livio's care at 5:12 PM, on 16 June 1904, and he became one of the 1.285 million immigrants who arrived in *L'America* during this year.

There is conflicting information about where Livio brought Nonno after meeting him at the pier on Ellis Island. The *Sardegna* ship manifest indicated that Nonno was to go to 66 Mulberry Street, noted for its crowded, uncomfortable, unhealthy conditions, and as a center for arriving Neapolitan immigrants.[38] However, other records

---

38. As a matter of fact, according to a ship manifest, Nonna Ettora's family stayed at 66 Mulberry Street in New York City when they arrived in 1907.

61

Waiting area in the Great Hall, Ellis Island.
— Photo in the public domain.

indicate that Nonno was escorted by his brother to 220 Sullivan Street.[39] Wherever he went, Nonno was lucky to have Livio to protect him from the chaos and poor living conditions that he had endured when he first arrived.

I am sure that Livio wanted to celebrate the arrival of his brother with a homecooked meal—the best that Nonno had had in thirteen days! I recall Livio having a fine reputation as an excellent cook of special Neapolitan dishes and delicacies.

Livio had some contacts in the garment industry so Nonno could "get his feet wet." But first, from his own experience, Livio knew what horrific conditions Nonno had endured in steerage, so he realized that Nonno needed to rest and get acclimated to the new environment before doing anything else.

---

39. My family never knew about Sullivan Street; we only knew about 66 Mulberry Street, so it is not clear where Nonno stayed when he first arrived.

Making a Living
Composing a Life

"To work he started the next morning
with an Italian laboring throng.
All of them looked so wan, so weary
to him, so rosy-cheeked and strong.
When that first day of work was ended
and he lay sleepless on his bed,
he missed his mother, missed his village
missed his childhood that was fled."
— JOSEPH TUSIANI[40]

When Nonno arrived in New York City, he was fortunate to have his brother Livio to support and help him adjust to his new life. Was Nonno homesick and did he have thoughts of returning to Contursi? Did he share his feelings with Livio or keep them private? As a teenager far away from home, how did he develop the strength to move on? What were his challenges? I can only speculate.

A Strong Work Ethic

First, he had to learn English to communicate, assimilate, and adapt to his new environment. I know that Nonno enrolled in night school to learn English. The Baxter Street School, a neighborhood public school not far from their residence on Sullivan Street,

---

40. Tusiani, *Gente Mia*, p. 31.

Nonno Totore is second from the left. Zio Livio is second from the right.
From the Cipolaro/Sorrentino Family Album, Courtesy of Rosanne Denaro.
Photo Restoration: Anthony Troiano @ Orazio Fotografik)

accommodated immigrants and their children. During the day, Nonno worked with Livio in the nearby garment district applying and perfecting his tailoring skills. At night he worked on perfecting his English skills.

Census records from 1910 to 1912 indicate that Nonno and his brother resided at 45 Greenwich Avenue. With the help and guidance of his older brother, Nonno was able to advance from apprentice tailor to finished tailor within several years of his arrival. In 1911, according to the U. S. Department of Labor, tailors' average weekly earnings was $13.83[41] (approximately $436 per week in 2023 dollars).

From 1913 to 1914, Livio and Nonno owned their own tailor shop, Cipollaro Bros. Tailors, at 46 Greenwich Avenue (photo above).

---

41. $435.53, 3.13% average annual inflation rate, cumulative price increase of 3,049.16% from 1911 to 2023. https://babel.hathitrust.org/cgi/pt?id=uc1.321060-20105729&view=1up&seq=10. https://www.in2013dollars.com/us/inflation/1911.

64

I wonder why their business was so short-lived, only one year? Could it be because of threats by the *"Mano Nera,"* the "Black Hand," a criminal organization in the early 20th century, plaguing, extorting, and victimizing honest immigrant Italian businessmen, and promising "protection" at an exorbitant cost?[42] Like their ordeals in steerage, neither Nonno nor Livio ever shared their brief business ownership experiences.

During his early years in *L'America,* Nonno distinguished himself as a custom tailor with Twyeffort, Inc., at 580 Fifth Avenue, a well-established upscale firm in Manhattan, originally located at 253 Fifth Avenue. It was founded by Emil Twyeffort and Jules Vinot in 1885, and subsequently owned by Twyeffort's debonaire son, Raymond Godfrey, who served as president of the National Association of Merchant Tailors in 1937.[43] I know that work was very important to Nonno, and he took pride in his final products. Nonno continued with the firm for approximately fifty years, until his retirement in the mid-1950s. During his tenure

©
TWYEFFORT, Inc.
580 5th AVENUE
NEW YORK

Twyeffort advertisement illustrating the elegance of formal wear, early-mid 20th Century.

---

42. Black Hand reference See Tomasi; Antonio Nicaso in Connell and Pugliese.

43. *The New York Times,* February 17, 1937.

Frances R. Curcio

at Twyeffort, formal men's wear became important in the "Roaring '20s." It was a very lucrative time to be a custom tailor when men's clothing and appearance reflected prosperity. Paying attention to how Nonno dressed, I believe that he subscribed to Twyeffort's philosophy: "Dressing correctly provides an emotional variety, well-balanced, of humor, dignity, joy, sorrow."[44]

As part of formal attire, the collar of the white shirt was removable for frequent and easy laundering. It wasn't until the "Roaring '20s," actually 1921, that Van Heusen developed the attached collar. Although Raymond Twyeffort was known to prefer the detached collar,[45] Nonno must have kept abreast of all new design and style developments. Perhaps the attached collar influenced Nonno's waistcoat and vest creations and structure. Unfortunately, there are no photographs illustrating Nonno's creations.

Once he was living on Staten Island after 1916, several times a week, Nonno would take the South Beach train to the Staten Island Ferry to travel from his home and shop into Manhattan. Then he would probably take the "R" subway train to 48th Street, and walk to Twyeffort's to pick up his assignment, complete any required measurements, fit clients, and finally, deliver a completed suit.

Attentive to detail, Nonno's work was so highly valued by Twyeffort that out of the sixty tailors employed, Nonno was the one who was entrusted and assigned to make suits for General Dwight D. Eisenhower, who later served as the 34th President of the United States; Pierre S. duPont, president of General Motors and member of the founding board of directors of the Empire State Building, which was the tallest building in the world when it opened in 1931; Horace Dodge, automobile manufacturing pioneer who may have influenced Nonno in owning Dodge cars; Henry J. Kaiser, father of modern American shipbuilding, who supplied the Liberty Fleet of cargo ships

---

44. *The New Yorker*, 1933, p. 12.

45. Beckman, "Men as Colorful as their Autos."

during World War II; and Babe Ruth, the famous slugger who spent 15 out of 22 seasons with the New York Yankees.

Although written more than 60 years after Nonno retired, Yoshimi Hasegawa captured the essence of the work of an excellent tailor: "The best painters are no different from the best tailors. Proportion, balance, colour. There's an aesthetic behind everything."[46] I may be partial, but I believe that Nonno's work was the epitome of these characteristics.

Nonno would toil in his shop behind his house on his neatly manicured property on Tompkins Avenue, Staten Island. Nonna, an asthmatic, did as much as she could to assist him. They both worked hard. They were frugal, they saved money, and they were able to furnish their house with fine monogrammed linens, china, crystal glassware, and elegant monogrammed silverware—all symbols of success. Displaying themselves and their possessions exemplified the notion of *fare bella figura*.[47] It is beyond simply "looking good." It is how they represented their achievements. Holidays and special occasions brought their extended family together as they enjoyed multi-course meals in their dining room—a showcase and testament to their ascension into the middle class.[48]

Strong Family Ties and Values

After leaving Contursi, Nonno dedicated his initial time in New York to developing his professional skills and reputation. Several years passed before Nonno would see his childhood acquaintance, Ettora, again. On March 18, 1907, at the age of 14, she arrived with her mother and her four siblings at Ellis Island on the 20-year-old Spanish Compania Transatlantic steamship, *Buenos Aires*. Her father, Enrico, arrived previously with his eldest son, Enrico, and arranged for the

---

46. Hasegawa, *Italian Tailoring*, p. 127.

47. Sciorra, *Italian Folk*.

48. Clark, "The Vision of the Dining Room."

family to live in the tenement at 66 Mulberry Street, the same address that appeared on the ship manifest when Nonno arrived in 1904.

Fulfilling the agreement between the two families back in Contursi, Nonno married Ettora on August 31, 1913, at St. Joseph's Church, Rosebank, Staten Island. Her entire family attended the wedding. Nonno and his bride moved to 948 Second Avenue between 50th and 51st Streets, where their first child, Amedeo was born on October 6, 1914. They lived in Manhattan until 1916, when Enrico finished building his house at 129 Richmond Avenue,[49] Arrochar, the north shore of Staten Island.

While in New York City, Enrico and other Contursians, including Nonno and Livio, became familiar with Staten Island, the most rural, bucolic, and at the time, the most Contursi-like of the five

Nonna Ettora and Nonno Totore's Wedding Photo.
— Cipolaro/Curcio Family Album.

---

49. Renamed McClean Avenue in 1930.

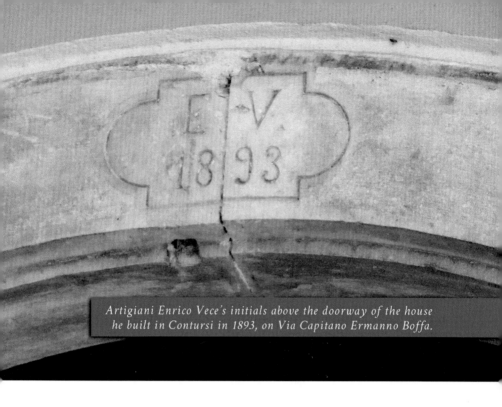

Artigiani Enrico Vece's initials above the doorway of the house he built in Contursi in 1893, on Via Capitano Ermanno Boffa.

boroughs. They would take the five-cent ride[50] on the Staten Island Ferry and then pay an additional five-cents to take the train to explore different parts of the Island. One route was to South Beach. Enrico, Nonno, and Livio took advantage of the opportunity to purchase land not too far from the beach. A builder in Contursi (see photo above of his initials on his house in Contursi), Enrico applied his skills on Staten Island, building three houses on Richmond Avenue, and the house on Tompkins Avenue for Nonno and his eldest daughter Ettora.

Enrico built his two-story house on Richmond Avenue first. While he was building his house, his wife, Bisnonna Antoinetta, and their children Enrico, Agostino, Maria, Gino, Romolo, and Filomena, lived in Manhattan at 66 Mulberry Street. Their eldest daughter, Ettora, my Nonna, lived in Manhattan with Nonno and their son, Amedeo. By 1916, Enrico's house was built. Three years after they were married, Nonno and Nonna moved into the upstairs apartment in her

---

50. The fare remained at five cents from the late 1890s until 1948, when it increased 100% to ten cents.

father's house.[51] It was the year that Nonni's second son, Enrico, was born on July 15. On May 6, 1919, their third child, a girl, Margherita, was born. Their fourth child, also a girl, Antoinetta, was born in 1921. She contracted pneumonia and died in 1922.

From the time he started working, Nonno saved money so he could own a house and provide for his family. He found a .23-acre plot of land up the street from his in-laws. According to *The New York Herald*, May 8, 1921, the value of a quarter-of-an acre of land was about $2,500 on the north shore, in contrast to $100 for the same size property on the south shore, a substantial amount in 1921 dollars ($41,784 in 2023 dollars).[52]

Nonno and Nonna's children: Amedeo, Margherita (Margaret), and Enrico (Henry). Taken at 1101 Tompkins Avenue; June 1928.
— Cipolaro/Curcio Family Album.

---

51. Although documents available online indicate that Enrico's two-story family dwelling was built in 1925, this conflicts with birth records of Nonno's children who were born in Enrico's house as early as 1916.

52. Adjusted for inflation, with the average annual inflation rate between 1921 and 2023 at 2.8%; with cumulative price increase of 1,571%).

Mio Nonno Totore and The American Dream

In 1922, a bittersweet year, after losing his baby daughter, Nonno was granted his American citizenship. It was also the year he and his family moved into the newly constructed house on Tompkins Avenue, built by his father-in-law. The two-floor house was spacious with room for a growing family. The main floor had front and back porches, a dining room, a living room, a kitchen, and a washroom. The second floor housed four bedrooms and a bathroom with indoor plumbing. The unfinished basement was used for storage. Originally, the house was designed with gaslights, but with the advent of electricity on Staten Island in the late nineteenth century the gaslights were eventually converted to electric lights.

The house was surrounded by enough property for *una sartoria*, a detached tailor shop in the back yard where Nonno worked; *una autorimessa*, a garage, where Nonno kept *la sua macchina*, his car; *un orto*, a vegetable garden where they planted vegetables; and a gazebo where the family would enjoy lunch and dinner during the summer months. Even after the children arrived and she had to manage a new house, Nonna, an accomplished seamstress, often assisted Nonno.

They had a radio that the family listened to together. I was told that my Nonna loved to listen to Milton Berle. When Berle moved to perform on television, the family enjoyed watching his facial expressions—which they could not see on the radio.

Another form of evening family entertainment was playing the player piano, also called the pianola, popular in the early twentieth century. My mother told me that she used to love to "play" it. There were no musicians in the family so the player piano was a perfect generator of music for sing-alongs. Nonno's in-laws also had player pianos. According to Michael Stinnett, founder and director of sales and historical archives at The Antique Piano Shop,[53] one of the typical manufacturers was Gulbransen, with prices ranging from the low-end Community Model, in mahogany, green, and golden oak, at $398, to the high-end White House model, $700, each with a ten-year guar-

---

53. www.antiquepianoshop.com; personal communication, 17 September 2022.

antee. My guess is that Nonno and his in-laws purchased the low-end Community Model for $398. This was a significant amount of money for a family during this time, as it was equivalent to about $7088 in 2023 dollars.[54] Most likely, Nonno had piano rolls for some of the most popular songs of the period (e.g., Al Jolson's "Swanee," "When You're Smiling," "Five-Foot-Two Eyes of Blue"). The great feature of the pneumatic player piano is that anyone who could reach the treadles with his/her foot could "make" music by pumping air into the system allowing the hammers to strike the strings to make sounds. Production of player pianos lost popularity with the advent of record players and radio and essentially ceased when the stock market crashed in 1929.

Once they had a radio, Nonno and his family enjoyed listening to the New York Philharmonic's live radio broadcasts under the baton of the great Italian maestro, Arturo Toscanini. Ed Sullivan, Dinah Shore, Danny Kaye, Burns and Allen, Hopalong Cassidy, the Lone Ranger all found their way into Nonno's living room, first via the radio and then via the television.

Owning a Car

Nonno's house had a detached *autorimessa*. I do not know when the garage was built or whether he owned a car before 1946, but family photos show family members near a car on trips to Bear Mountain, New York; Cherry Hill, New Jersey; and the Jersey shore. When Nonno had the opportunity to design and create custom suits for Horace Elgin Dodge Jr., I imagine that Nonno inquired about Dodge automobiles. Was he given a discount? Most likely not, but deciding to purchase a Dodge may have been related to making suits for Mr. Dodge and meeting him for fittings. In 1946, the four-door Dodge cost about $1,200 (about $18,411 in 2023 dollars). He loaned the car to my father to go with my mother on their honeymoon in the Pocono Mountains in 1948 (see photo on following page).

---

54. Annual inflation over this period was 2.89%.

Nonno's daughter, Margaret, posing near Nonno's 1946 Dodge by the Pocono Mountains; July 1948.

Nonno and Nonna were blessed to witness the marriages of their children: In 1944, Amedeo married Virginia, whose parents were from Contursi; in 1947, Henry married Mildred, whose parents were from Salerno and a commune near Naples; and in 1948, Margaret married Raffaele, whose parents were from the Neapolitan communes of Scafati and Castellemmare di Stabia. Over the years, six grandchildren were welcomed into the family.

Amedeo and Virginia, November 19, 1944.

Frances R. Curcio

Mildred and Henry, April 12, 1947.

Margaret and Raffaele, July 11, 1948.

Mio Nonno Totore and The American Dream

Nonna was only sixty years old in 1952, when she needed a gall bladder operation. Although this procedure was not very common at the time, the operation was not expected to be life threatening. Throughout her life, Nonna had suffered with asthma, so she had health issues. During the procedure, her family patiently waited in the hospital for news about her condition. When the family doctor entered the waiting room, he blurted out callously and bluntly that "She died on the table." He followed this announcement with: "She was an old asthmatic anyway." I can imagine how shocked and grief-stricken everyone must have been. These insensitive words spoken by a *paesano*, a fellow Italian countryman, were embedded in the memories of my grieving parents and relatives. The piercing words have sadly stayed with me. It is unfathomable that a family physician could be so heartless and unsympathetic. Needless to say, this was a sad and difficult time for the family.

By 1954, my father completed building our house on a corner plot adjacent to Nonno's and we all moved in together. For about one year, Nonno rented his house. He was unable to watch what abusive tenants were doing to his house, so he put the house on the market. He sold it in 1955 for $50,000 ($620,685 in 2023 dollars).

75

Realizing the American Dream

*"What is so enchanting as the American
Dream? To be possessed of that Dream
presupposes that, like St. Paul, one must be
obedient to the vision splendid."*
— EDGAR DEWITT JONES[55]

When Nonno arrived in New York in 1904, he had no valuables, but he had his values. He came with his whole "new" life ahead of him as he left behind his "old" young life. I often wonder how sad, *triste* he must have been to leave behind his former short life, his family, friends, and all things familiar. What dreams, *i sogni*, and aspirations, *le aspirazioni* could a fourteen-year-old have had in Contursi when at the time, educational and employment opportunities were limited? Did he bring any of those *sogni* and *aspirazioni* with him to America? At fourteen years of age, Nonno's dreams may have been temporary and short-lived. Most likely new dreams and aspirations evolved as he began to adjust and assimilate to the new environment while working during the day, learning English at night, and composing his new life.

The term, "the American Dream," had not yet been coined in 1904, but the concept had been around since the first settlers in the New World left their homes in the Old World and arrived in the land of hope. Everyone who ventured to the New World brought their *aspirazioni*, their *sogni*. It was not until 1931 that the term "the American

---

55. Jones, *The Influence of Henry Clay*, p. 38.

Dream" appeared in *The Epic of America*, by James Truslaw Adams, who described the "dream of a land in which life should be better and richer and fuller for every man [and woman], with opportunity for each according to ability or achievement."[56] For some it was the dream of religious freedom and liberty; for others it was the dream of political freedom, equality, and democracy; for many it was to improve the prospects of a productive and rewarding life for themselves and their progeny. What could a fourteen-year-old's dream have been? Whatever it was, achieving it was not easy, especially for Italian immigrants who were despised and not welcomed in America.[57] It required hard work, determination, stamina, and a will to survive. Italian immigrants were faced with challenges and obstacles created by negative attitudes, biases, and prejudice towards them not only by members of other ethnic groups, but by politicians and the press as well, making it difficult to be "obedient to the vision splendid." Like many immigrants before and after them, they "never gave in to grievance and hate,"[58] they persevered to overcome all odds.

Why were President Theodore Roosevelt and Senator Henry Cabot Lodge, among others, outspoken critics of Italian immigrants? Was it because Italians were not of the believed-to-be superior Aryan race characterized by Proto-Indo-European heritage? Was it because the Italians were viewed as having inferior intelligence because they did not have the opportunity to go to school in the old country? Was it because when they arrived they were unable to speak English? Was it because they were willing to work for very little money and take jobs away from American citizens, who were in their "same shoes" not so long before? The hard working, determined Italian immigrants proved Roosevelt, Lodge, and the others wrong. They were strong physically and mentally. On the one hand, as the Italian immigrants proved them-

---

56. Truslaw, p. 404.

57. Stapinski, "When America Barred Italians."

58. Astor, "Firsts, Flags and Reversals," p. A15.

selves to be valuable contributors to building the country, President Roosevelt's negative attitude towards them seemed to wane. Was his change in attitude towards the Italians in his political interest or was he sincere? On the other hand, Senator Lodge's promotion of racial stereotypes of Italian immigrants spilled over into the general public and into the press, demeaning the immigrants and adding to the difficulty of their achieving the American Dream.

However, despite roadblocks, many Italian immigrants were successful in surviving and prospering. Their inability to speak English did not interfere with their use of brawn to contribute to building and shaping America—the infrastructure—roads, railways, tunnels, bridges, reservoirs, dams, pumping stations, all of the facilities required for towns, cities, and the country to function effectively and efficiently. There were also the skilled immigrant workers, like Nonno, who helped "dress" American businessmen and politicians for success. They influenced fashion and promoted style.

Based on Nonno's words and deeds, *nelle sue parole e nelle sue azioni,* it was obvious that he had a strong commitment, *forte impegno,* to his faith, *la sua fede,* and to his new, adoptive country, *il suo paese adottivo.* For Nonno, realizing the American Dream was beyond such material things as owning a house, *una casa,* and a car, *una macchina.* Nonno was able to take advantage of the ideals of freedom, *libertà,* democracy, *democrazia,* equality, *uguaglianza* and justice for all, *giustizia per tutti.* He shaped his own destiny even when his dream may have seemed unreachable or impossible during his early years in America.

Nonno lived and realized an American Dream, *his* American Dream. While working for Twyeffort, he established himself as a sought-after custom tailor. He had settled in a comfortably furnished new house with his family. He had "things." He had the means to purchase "things." He was proud to be living in the land of opportunity, despite the hardships that he faced to earn what he had. Did Nonno want to return to Italy as soon as possible? Once he married, had children, and was settled in his newly adoptive country, he obviously decided to stay.

I often wonder whether Nonno had some regrets that living the American Dream may have eroded the original values, traditions, and beliefs that he brought with him. As he adjusted to American ideals, he did not revert to the "old" ways of his father: He did not select spouses for his children, and he did not dictate his son's occupations. He always seemed to be content with his children's choices.

As his children became Americanized, their primary language was English, not Italian. Although the family spoke the Neapolitan dialect at home, in school and at work, they spoke English. Nonno valued and subscribed to the American ideal of education for all. Education opened the doors of success not only for his children, but for his grandchildren as well. The close-knit family remained the center of their lives as they attempted to maintain their values and cultural traditions.

Early in the 20th century, festivals were held celebrating San Donato, patron saint of Contursi and San Rocco, patron saint of Lioni, among others. As the older folks died, so too did many of the traditional festivities. For example, by the end of the 1950s, the feast of San Donato was no longer celebrated on Staten Island. As time passed, immigrants, their children, and grandchildren continued to adjust, assimilate, and make accommodations. They were Americanized. No doubt Nonno witnessed the younger generations drifting away from tradition. I wonder how this made him feel. He had to accept what becoming an American did to him and to his family.

Nonno's dreams were realized in his accomplishments, his children, and his grandchildren. I can imagine the feeling of satisfaction he must have experienced as he presided over holiday dinners, special parties, and events, as he watched his family grow and thrive. I feel blessed to have had the opportunity to have Nonno in my life for twenty-two years. The special love and bond created from the formative years are treasured memories never to be forgotten. I can attest to the fact that the joy and benefits of living with a grandparent cannot be understated. Grandparents are a link to rich family history. Grandchildren who live with their grandparents reap the benefits of wisdom,

Mio Nonno Totore and The American Dream

experience, and special bonding to help them connect with the past and build a life for the future.[59]

Was it easy for Nonno to leave his familiar surroundings, his family, and his friends? Of course not. Was it necessary? Perhaps it was, at the time. Nonno and his brothers left Contursi, but other siblings stayed and composed productive, happy lives. Similar to Lin Manuel Miranda's musings,[60] I often ask myself, what if Nonno had stayed in Italy and never came to America? Who would I be if I grew up in Contursi-Terme? After visiting the commune many times in the past twelve years and interacting with my newly found relatives, I realize that our similarities are much greater than our differences. When I visit, I feel as though I am going home.

---

59. Kaufman, "Generations Shrink a Gap as Roommates."

60. Aguilar, "Helping a Dream 'Find Its Way'."

"Questa è la Fine"

As I think about life's happy occasions and sad moments, I try to savor the joyful memories and minimize thoughts of sorrow. However, as I contemplate and record all of my pleasant memories of Nonno, I am always left with the reality of a sad ending.

I will never forget returning home from teaching on a gloomy, frigid Thursday afternoon, January 17, 1974, to find my mother crying. She told me that she took Nonno to pick up his new eyeglasses and as he was getting into the passenger side of the car in the parking lot, he did not notice the black ice. He slipped and fell. He was unable to get up. My mother struggled to try to help him get up, but she did not have the strength to lift him. A man passing by offered to help. He lifted Nonno, put him in the car, and walked away. After Nonno was settled in his seat, as my mother started to close the car door, he grabbed the door and looking her squarely in the eyes he said, *"Questa è la fine,"* this is the end. She told me that she gave him encouragement and that he would be O.K. She closed the door, got into the driver's seat and, seeking her brother's help, she drove Nonno to the Ocean Sweet Shoppe. My Uncle Amedeo then drove him to the hospital. Nonno broke his hip. He needed surgery. The good news is: The operation was a success. The bad news is: He never recovered.

Did he give up? Was he tired of living? Was he worried about being a burden to his children and grandchildren? It was devastating to watch. What could the doctors do for him if he chose not to cooperate? My family and I would visit him every day, but he did not have the energy (or the will) to speak. After lingering for a little more than two weeks, he died on Sunday, February 3rd, the Feast of St. Blaise. He was laid to rest on Wednesday, February 5, 1974, near his wife, Ettorina, and their baby, Antoinetta.

In the end, Nonno may have felt as though his life was over. No way—he's still in my heart and he continues to be the firm and steady trunk supporting the branches of a thriving family tree. I am comforted by the words of Joseph Tusiani:[61]

> "It does not matter what you say, what tongue
> you speak, what saint or demon you invoke:
> you're not America but she is you—
> a bond of force and faith,
> a chain of love and loss.
> You'll be tomorrow the surviving throng,
> the roots and still the branches of the oak,
> the antiquated and therefore the new,
> the life that springs of death,
> the ore that comes of dross."

---

61. Tusiani, *Gente Mia*, p. 14.

Selected Bibliography

Adams, James Truslow. *The Epic of America*. Harbor, FL: Simon Publications, 2001/1931.

Aguilar, Carlos. "Helping a Dream 'Find Its Way'," *The New York Times*, 12 June 2021, pp. C1, C6.

Algier, Horatio Jr. *The Collected Complete Work of Horatio Alger*. Kindle Edition, n.d.

Astor, Maggie. "Firsts, Flags and Reversals: A Look at Haley's Résumé." *The New York Times*, February 15, 2023, p. A15.

Banfield, Edward C. *The Moral Basis of a Backward Society*. New York: The Free Press, 1958.

Barker, Christian. "The History and Anatomy of Neapolitan Tailoring." https://therake.com/stories/craft/the-history-and-anatomy-of-neapolitan-tailoring/, n.d.

Barone, Adam. "American Dream." Retrieved on January 29, 2021 from https://www.investopedia.com/terms/a/american-dream.asp.

Basile, Giambattista. *The Tale of Tales, or Entertainment for Little Ones* (trans. by Nancy L. Canepa). Detroit, MI: Wayne State University Press, 2016.

Beckman, Frank. "Men as Colorful as their Autos." *Detroit Free Press*, May 20 1955, p. 13.

Benanti, Carol Ann. "Digging Deeper: Staten Island Resident Frances R. Curcio Continues Search for Family Roots." *Staten Island Advance*, 7 November 2014. https://www.silive.com/inside_out_column/2014/11/fran.html

Benanti, Carol Ann. "Bridging Two Worlds: A Dream Comes True for Arrochar Resident who Researched her Italian Roots." *The Staten Island Advance*, 7 August, 2022, p. A26. https://www.silive.com/entertainment/2022/08/bridging-two-worlds-a--dream-comes-true-for- arrochar-resident-who-researched-her-italian-roots-inside-out.html

Blake, Ilona M. "For My Grandpa." *Family Friend Poems,* 2006. Retrieved from https://www.familyfriendpoems.com/print/poem/MjAwNDU=

Bloom, Harold. (Ed.). *Bloom's Literary Themes: The American Dream.* New York: Infobase Publishing, 2009.

Borzellino, Giuseppe. *Contursi Terme: Cenni Storici Fino al 1750.* Contursi: Pro-Loco e Centro di Cultura Popolare U.N.L.A., 1976.

Cabrini, Frances Xavier. *To the Ends of the Earth: The Missionary Travels of Frances X. Cabrini.* Staten Island, NY: The Center for Migration Studies of New York, Inc., 2001/1902.

Campania: A Land as Clear as Daylight. Naples, Italy: Gruppo Pubbitat, 2007.

Cannato, Vincent J. *American Passage: The History of Ellis Island.* New York: Harper Perennial, 2010.

Clark, Clifford E. "The Vision of the Dining Room: Plan Book Dreams and Middle-Class Realities." In Kathryn Grover (Ed.), *Dining in America: 1850-1900* (pp. 142-172). Amherst, MA: University of Massachusetts Press, 1987. https://archive.org/details/dininginamerica10000unse/page/168/mode/2up?view=theater

Connell, William J., & Stanislao G. Pugliese (Eds.). *The Routledge History of Italian Americans.* New York: Routledge, 2018.

Covello, Leonard. *Social Background of the Italo-American School Child: A Study of the Southern Italian Family Mores and Their Effect on the School Situation in Italy and America.* Totowa, New Jersey: Rowman and Littlefield, 1972.

Covello, Leonard, with Guido D'Agostino. *The Heart is the Teacher.* New York: John D. Calandra Institute, 2013/1958.

Cullen, Jim. *The American Dream: A Short History of an Idea that Shaped a Nation.* New York: Oxford University Press, 2003.

Curcio, Frances R. "Island Family Sets Off on Search for Its Italian Roots." *The Staten Island Advance,* 19 October 2011. https://www.silive.com/eastshore/2011/10/island_family_sets_off_on_sear.html

Curcio, Frances R. "Arrochar Resident Makes Some Surprising Discoveries about Family's Roots during Recent Trip to Italy." *The Staten Island Advance,* 18 July 2012. https://www.silive.com/eastshore/2012/07/arrochar_resident_makes_some_s.html

D'Angelo, Pascal. *Son of Italy.* Toronto: Guernica, 2003/1924.

Dickie, John. *Darkest Italy.* New York: St. Martin's Press, 1999.

Dillingham, William Paul. *Reports of the Immigration Commission.* Washington, DC: Government Printing Office, 1911.

Dupont, Brandon, Drew Keeling, and Thomas Weiss. *Passenger Fares for Overseas Travel in the 19th and 20th Centuries.* Paper presented at Annual Meeting of the Economic History Association, Vancouver, Canada, September 2012. https://eh.net/eha/wp-content/uploads/2013/11/Weissetal.pdf

Durante, Francesco, ed. *Italoamericana: The Literature of the Great Migration, 1880-1943.* New York: Fordham University Press, 2014.

Eiselein, Gregory. (Ed.). *Emma Lazarus: Selected Poems and Other Writings.* Ontario, Canada: Broadview Press, 2002.

Foerster, R. F. *The Italian Emigration of Our Times.* Cambridge, MA: Harvard University Press, 1919.

Gambino, Richard. *Blood of my Blood: The Dilemma of the Italian-Americans.* Cheektowaga, NY: Guernica Editions, Inc., 1996.

Gardaphé, Fred L. *Dagoes Read: Tradition and the Italian/American Writer.* Toronto, Canada: Guernica Editions, Inc., 1996.

Gardaphé, Fred L. *Italian Signs, American Streets.* Durham, NC: Duke University Press, 1996.

Gardaphé, Fred L. *Leaving Little Italy.* Albany, NY: State University of New York Press, 2004.

Gillan, Maria Mazziotta. *Ancestors' Song.* New York: Bordighera Press, 2013.

Giura, Maria. *What My Father Taught Me.* New York: Bordighera Press, 2018.

Glazer, Nathan, and Daniel Patrick Moynihan. *Beyond the Melting Pot: The Negroes, Puerto Ricans, Jews, Italians, and Irish of New York City.* Cambridge, MA: The M.I.T. Press and Harvard University Press, 1963.

Golbe, Lawrence I., Giuseppe DiOrio, Giuseppe Sanges, Alice M. Lazzarini, Salvatore La Sala, Vincenzo Bonavita, and Roger C. Duvoisin. "Clinical Genetic Analysis of Parkinson's Disease in the Contursi Kindred." *Annals of Neurology 40,* no. 5 (November 1966): 767-775.

Golbe, Lawrence I., Giuseppe DiOrio, Alice Lazzarini, Peter Vieregge, Oscar S. Gershanik, Vincenzo Bonavita, and Roger C. Duvoisin. "The Contursi Kindred, A Large Family with Autosomal Dominant Parkinson's Disease: Implications of Clinical and Molecular Studies." *Advances in Neurology 80,* (1999): 165-170.

Grant, Madison. *The Passing of the Great Race or The Racial Basis of European History,* 4th Revised Edition. New York: Charles Scribner's Sons, 1936.

Hasegawa, Yoshimi. *Italian Tailoring: A Glimpse into the World of Sartorial Masters.* Milano, Italy: Skira editore, 2018.

Hawley, Joshua David. *Theodore Roosevelt: Preacher of Righteousness.* New Haven, CT: Yale University Press, 2008.

Iamurri, Gabriel A. *The True Story of An Immigrant.* Boston, MA: The Christopher Publishing House, 1951.

"The Italian Tailors of Naples." *The Italian Tribune,* 20 June 2019, 1, 4.

Jacobson, Marion. *Squeeze This! A Cultural History of the Accordion in America.* Urbana, IL: University of Illinois Press, 2012.

Jones, Edgar DeWitt. *The Influence of Henry Clay upon Abraham Lincoln.* Lexington, KY: The Henry Clay Memorial Foundation, 1952.

Kaufman, Joanne. "Generations Shrink a Gap as Roommates." *The New York Times,* 2 October 2022, RE9.

Kennedy, John F. *A nation of immigrants.* New York: Harper Perennial, 2018/1964.

LaGumina, Salvatore J. *The Immigrants Speak: Italian Americans Tell Their Story.* New York: Center for Migration Studies, 1979.

LaGumina, Salvatore J.. *From Steerage to Suburbs: Long Island Italians.* NY: Wiley, 1988. Retrieved from http://onlinelibrary.wiley.com/doi/10.1111/cms3.1988.6.issue-1/issuetoc

LaSorte, Michael. *La Merica: Images of Italian Greenhorn Experiences.* Philadelphia, PA: Temple University Press, 1985.

Laurino, Maria. *Were You Always an Italian? Ancestors and Other Icons of Italian America.* New York: W. W. Norton & Company, 2000.

Leng, Charles W., and William T. Davis. *Staten Island and Its People: A History, 1609-1929.* Staten Island, NY: Lewis Historical Publishing Company, 1930.

Lord, Eliot, John J. D. Trenor, and Samuel June Barrows. *The Italian in America.* Freeport, NY: Books for Libraries Press, 1970/1905.

Mangione, Jerre, & Ben Morreale. *La Storia: Five Centuries of the Italian American Experience.* New York: Harper, 1992.

Marshall, Alex. "Passion for Acting Shifts to Food." *The New York Times,* October 5, 2021, C1, 2.

Masella, Aristide B. *Le Avventure di Giovanni Passaguai.* New York: Holt, Rinehart and Winston, 1941.

Matteo, Thomas W. *Then & Now: Staten Island.* Charleston, SC: Arcadia Publishing, 2006.

Matteo, Thomas W. *Staten Island: I Didn't Know That!* Virginia Beach, VA: The Donning Company Publishers, 2007.

McCormack, John, with Alfonso Cipolla and Alessandro Napoli. *The Italian Puppet Theater: A History.* Jefferson, NC: McFarland & Company, Inc., Publishers, 2010.

Musmanno, Michael A. *The Story of the Italians in America.* Garden City, New York: Doubleday & Company, 1965.

Napoli, Joseph. *A Dying Cadence: Memories of a Sicilian Childhood.* W. Bethesda, MD: Marna Press, 1986.

The New York Times. "Trade Boom Due Tailors are Told," 17 February 1937, p. 39.

Pignata, Franco. *Il Sentiero dei Passi Perduti.* Contursi Terme, Italia: La Fonte di Contursi Terme, 2007.

Pignata, Vito Nello. *Contursi Terme: Storia Fotografica dal 1865 al 1983.* Salerno, Italy: Editore Boccia, 1984.

Paolocelli, Paul. *Under the Southern Sky: Stories of the Real Italy and the Americans who it Created.* New York: St. Martin's Press, 2003.

Regione Campania and Comune di Contursi Terme. *Contursi Terme: Tra Storia e Natura.* Italia: Edizione Artecnica Production—Mediart, 2003.

Riis, Jacob A. *How the Other Half Lives.* Garden City, NY: Dover Publications, 1971/1901.

Risen, Clay. "Who owns Theodore Roosevelt?" *The New York Times,* 28 July 2019, p. SR3.

Saladini, Sr., Vincent Rocco. *The Tailor's Thread: An Italian-American Legacy.* Bloomington, IN: AuthorHouse, 2003.

Samuel, Lawrence R. *The American Dream: A Cultural History.* Syracuse, NY: Syracuse University Press, 2012.

"Sartorial Splendor and Chat." *The New York Times,* 4 August 2019, p. 8 NJ.

Scelsa, Joseph V., Salvatore J. LaGumina, and Lydio Tomasi. *Italian Americans in Transition.* Staten Island, NY: The American Italian Historical Association, 1990.

Schiavo, Giovanni. *Four Centuries of Italian-American History.* New York: Center for Migration Studies, 1992.

Sciorra, Joseph. *Italian Folk: Vernacular Culture in Italian-American Lives.* New York: Fordham University Press, 2011.

Sherry, Virginia N. "Grassroots Research in Italy Continues for Staten Island Resident." *Staten Island Advance,* 1 August 2013. https://www.silive.com/eastshore/2013/08/grassroots_research_in_italy_c.html

Sloniowska, Zanna. "I Left Ukraine 20 Years Ago. But It Never Left Me." *The New York Times,* 9 March 2022, p. A21.

Stapinski, Helene. "When America Barred Italians." *The New York Times,* 2 June 2017, p. A25.

Stern, Bert. "Steerage." *Poetry,* 170 No. 3, (June 1997): 136-138.

"Talk of the Town: Beau Twyeffort." *The New Yorker,* 13 May 1933, pp. 12-13.

Tamburri, Anthony Julian. *The Columbus Affair: Imperatives for an Italian/American Agenda.* New Fairfield, CT: Casa Lago Press, 2021.

Tamburri, Anthony Julian, Paolo J. Giordano, and Fred L. Gardaphé, eds. *From the Margin: Writings in Italian Americana* (Rev. Ed.). West Lafayette, IN: Purdue University Press, 2000.

To Arrive at Ellis Island. Retrieved on 5 August 2022 from http://www.ellisisland.se/english/ellisisland_immigration2.asp

Tomasi, Lydio, ed. *The Italian in America: The Progressive View, 1891-1914.* New York: Center for Migration Studies, 1978.

Tucciarone, Joe, and Ben Lariccia. *Italians Swindled to New York: False Promises at the Dawn of Immigration.* Charleston, SC: The History Press, 2021.

Tusiani, Joseph. *Gente Mia and Other Poems.* Stone Park, IL: Italian Cultural Center, 1978.

Villari, Luigi. *Italian Life in Town and Country.* New York: G. P. Putnam's Sons, Knickerbocker Press, 1902.

Viscusi, Robert. *ellis island.* New York: Bordighera Press, 2012.

Waller, Edith. "The Italian Workmen of America to Americans." In Lydio Tomasi, ed. *The Italian in America: The Progressive View 1891-1914. NY:* Center for Migration Studies, 1978/1912-13, p. 287.

Westover, Tara. "I Am Not Proof of the American Dream." *The New York Times,* 6 February 2022, p. SR 10.

Williams, Phyllis H. *South Italian Folkways in Europe and America: A Handbook for Social Workers, Visiting Nurses, School Teachers, and Physicians.* New York: Russell & Russell, 1938.

Wong, Aliza. *Race and the Nation in Liberal Italy, 1861-1911: Meridionalism, Empire, and Diaspora.* New York: Pulgrave Macmillan, 2006.

Mio Nonno Totore and The American Dream

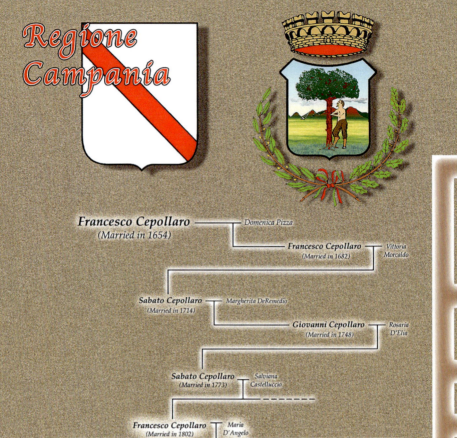
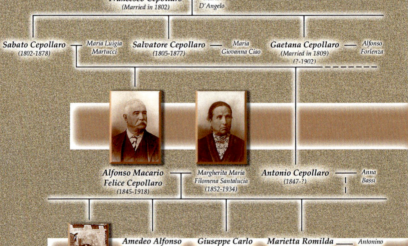

CEPOLLARO / CIPOLLARO / CIPOLARO FAMILY TREE

Comune di Contursi Terme

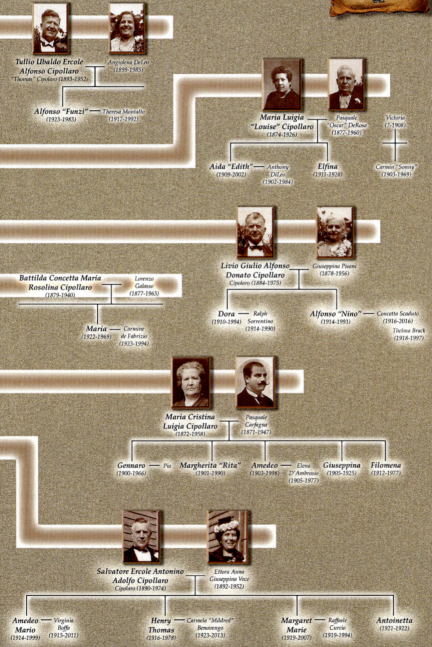

93

Appendix 1

Appendix 1

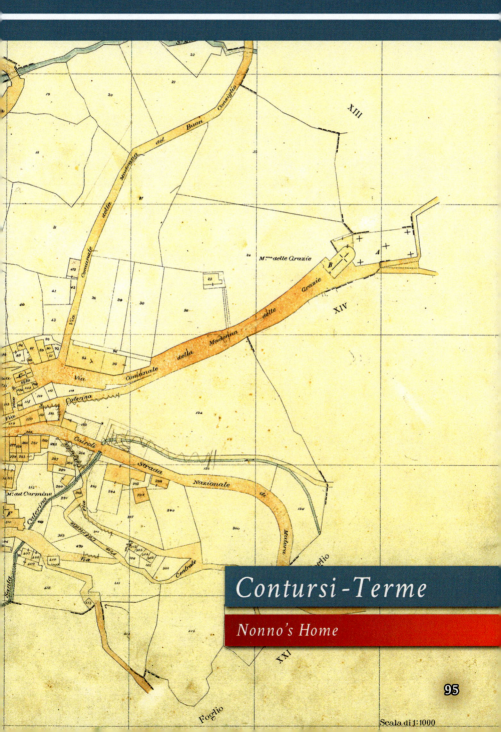

Contursi-Terme

Nonno's Home

Appendix 1

Appendix 1

View from Nonno's Window

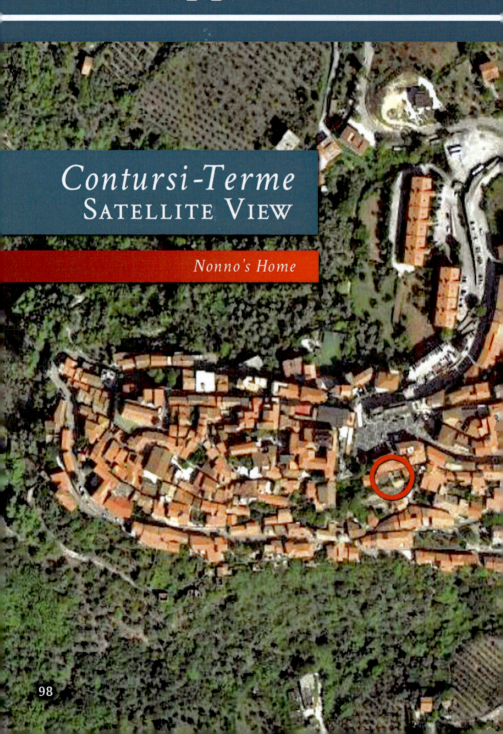

Appendix 1

Appendix 2

Original birth certificate for Salvatore (Cepollaro) Cipollaro.

Appendix 2

COMUNE DI CONTURSI TERME
PROVINCIA DI SALERNO

CERTIFICATO DI NASCITA

L'UFFICIALE DELLO STATO CIVILE

CERTIFICA

Che dal registro degli ATTI DI NASCITA di questo Comune dell'anno **1890** parte **I** SERIE /// NUMERO **28** risulta che il giorno **quattordici** del mese **Febbraio** dell'anno **MILLEOTTOCENTONOVANTA**

in **CONTURSI TERME**

è nato **CEPOLLARO Salvatore**.

In esenzione di bollo per uso consentito.

Dalla residenza Municipale lì 04/06/2019

L'UFFICIALE DI ANAGRAFE DELEGATO
Francesca Lenza

Piazza Garibaldi, 84024 Contursi Terme (SA) , Tel. 0828991013 Fax 0828991069
Part. Iva 01033260652 – cod. fiscale 82001930658 – www.comune.contursiterme.sa.it

Official version of Salvatore (Cepollaro) Cipollaro's birth certificate from the city of Contursi-Terme.

Appendix 3

Salvatore Cipollaro's Naturalization Papers: Declaration of Intent.

Appendix 3

Salvatore Cipollaro's Naturalization Papers: Oath of Allegiance.

Appendix 3

Salvatore Cipollaro's Naturalization Papers: Petition for Naturalization.

Appendix 4

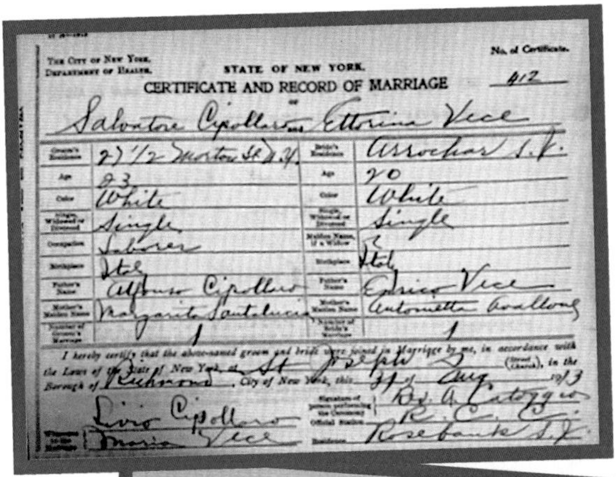

THE CITY OF NEW YORK.
DEPARTMENT OF HEALTH.

No. of Certificate. 412

STATE OF NEW YORK.

CERTIFICATE AND RECORD OF MARRIAGE

of

Salvatore Cipollaro and Ettorina Vece

Groom's Residence	27 1/2 Morton St. N.Y.	Bride's Residence	Arrochar S.I.
Age	23	Age	20
Color	White	Color	White
Single, Widowed or Divorced	Single	Single, Widowed or Divorced	Single
Occupation	Laborer	Maiden Name, if a Widow	
Birthplace	Italy	Birthplace	Italy
Father's Name	Alfonso Cipollaro	Father's Name	Enrico Vece
Mother's Maiden Name	Margarita Santalucia	Mother's Maiden Name	Antonetta Avallone
Number of Groom's Marriage	1	Number of Bride's Marriage	1

I hereby certify that the above-named groom and bride were joined in Marriage by me, in accordance with the Laws of the State of New York, at St Joseph's (Street, Church), in the Borough of Richmond, City of New York, this 31 of Aug 1913

Witnesses to the Marriage: Livio Cipollaro, Maria Vece

Signature of person performing the Ceremony: Rev. A. Catoggio

Official Station: R. C. C.

Residence: Rosebank S.I.

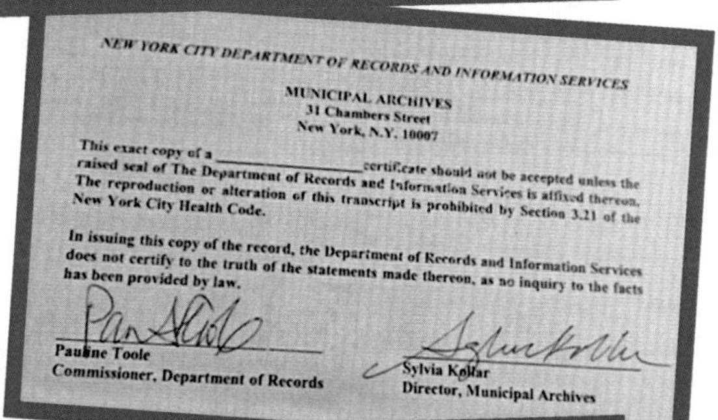

NEW YORK CITY DEPARTMENT OF RECORDS AND INFORMATION SERVICES

MUNICIPAL ARCHIVES
31 Chambers Street
New York, N.Y. 10007

This exact copy of a ____________ certificate should not be accepted unless the raised seal of The Department of Records and Information Services is affixed thereon. The reproduction or alteration of this transcript is prohibited by Section 3.21 of the New York City Health Code.

In issuing this copy of the record, the Department of Records and Information Services does not certify to the truth of the statements made thereon, as no inquiry to the facts has been provided by law.

Pauline Toole
Commissioner, Department of Records

Sylvia Kollar
Director, Municipal Archives

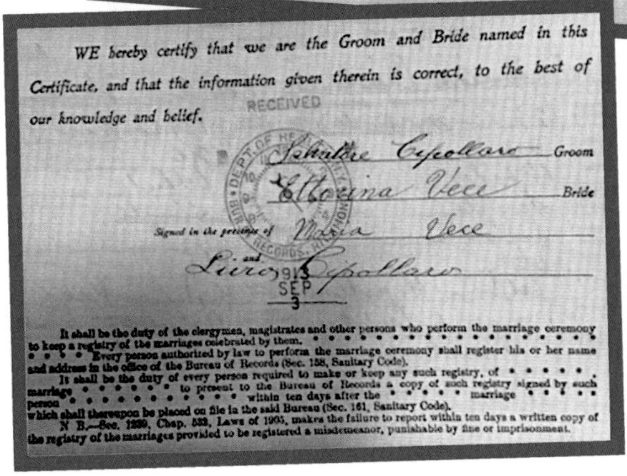

WE hereby certify that we are the Groom and Bride named in this Certificate, and that the information given therein is correct, to the best of our knowledge and belief.

RECEIVED

Salvatore Cipollaro Groom

Ettorina Vece Bride

Signed in the presence of Maria Vece

and Livio Cipollaro

DEPT. OF HEALTH RECORDS, RICHMOND 1913 SEP 3

It shall be the duty of the clergymen, magistrates and other persons who perform the marriage ceremony to keep a registry of the marriages celebrated by them. • Every person authorized by law to perform the marriage ceremony shall register his or her name and address in the office of the Bureau of Records (Sec. 158, Sanitary Code).

It shall be the duty of every person required to make or keep any such registry, of • • • • • • marriage • • • • • • to present to the Bureau of Records a copy of such registry signed by such person • • • • • • • • • • • within ten days after the • • • • • marriage • • • • • which shall thereupon be placed on file in the said Bureau (Sec. 161, Sanitary Code).

N. B.—Sec. 1239, Chap. 533, Laws of 1905, makes the failure to report within ten days a written copy of the registry of the marriages provided to be registered a misdemeanor, punishable by fine or imprisonment.

Marriage Documents.

Appendix 5

SCOPA

A Neapolitan Card Game

— 2 Players —

Values for Cards:
- King (Re): 10; Horseman (Cavallo): 9; Woman (Donna): 8
- Values 7-2 have a corresponding number of symbols.
- Ace (Asso): 1 — These cards have one fancy symbol for each suit.

Suits for Cards:
- Coin (Denaro); Sword (Spada); Club (Bastone); Cup (Coppa)

Rules:
- Four cards dealt in center, three cards dealt to each of the two players, alternating one card at each. Dealer remains the same for the whole round; alternating when round is over.
- Each player has a chance to match a card in the center; if there are options for making a sum, the unit card must be taken first.
- If a player takes all remaining cards in the center, the player sweeps the board (making a "Scopa" which is equal to 1 point).
- When the three cards for each player are used, the dealer gives each player three more cards in the same alternating fashion as the first round.
- The round continues until there are no cards left in the deck.
- At the end of the round, if there are cards left on the board, the last player to pick up cards will get what remains.
- Points are tallied up at the end of each round. The game is over when one player earns 11 points.
- The object of the game is to obtain the most points in each round to obtain 11 points before the other player.
- You can score points in each round in a few different ways. The first way is by "sweeping" the board of all cards (Scopa).

Appendix 5

Other ways to score points after each round ends:

- Obtain the most cards out of the two players — 1 Point.
    - If both players finish with 20 cards each, no point is awarded.
- Obtain the most Coin cards out of the two players – 1 Point.
    - If both players finish with 5 coin cards each, no point is awarded.
- Obtain the 7 of Coins Card (*Sette Bello* - The Beautiful Seven) - 1 Point.
- Obtain "*La Settanta*" — This is a total value from the highest cards from each suit that each player has for non-face cards. (7-Ace) 7 being the highest value.
    - All 7 Cards collected from one player is an automatic 1-point for the player who collects them.)

— 4 Players (Scopone) —

Rules:

- 4 Players play in teams of 2, sitting across from your partner.
- Each player is dealt 10 cards, to the left of the dealer, alternating between players and teams. Dealer alternates to the left when round is over.
- The player to the left of the dealer goes first, on a clear board to initiate the round of play. The second player can "sweep" the board if he can match the first player's card or just drop a random card.
- Round continues until there are no cards left by any player.
- At the end of the round, if there are cards left on the board, the last player to pick up cards will get what remains.
- If a player takes all remaining cards in the center, the player sweeps the board (making a "Scopa" which is equal to 1 point).
- Points are tallied up at the end of each round, the two teams add their cards and points as 1 team each. The game is over when one team earns 11 points.
- The object of the game is to obtain the most points in each round to obtain 11 points before the other player.

Other ways to score points is the same as the 2 player game.

Appendix 6

BRISCOLA
A Neapolitan Card Game

— 2 or More Players —

Cards, by Rank	Point Value
Ace (Asso)	11
Three (Tre)	10
King (Re)	4
Knight (Cavallo)	3
Woman (Donna)	2

Unlisted cards have no point value. In total, a deck has 120 points. The player with the most points accumulated wins.

- Shuffle the deck and deal each player three cards (if two players, give each 9 cards).
- Place the next card, the *Briscola* card (or the trump suit for the game) face up on the playing surface, and the remaining deck face down. (Sometimes the *Briscola* card is half covered by the rest of the deck.
- Deal and play the game in a counterclockwise direction. The player to the right of the dealer goes first by placing one card face up on the playing surface. In turn, each player reveals a card. The player who wins the hand is determined as follows:
  - if any *briscola* (trump) has been played, the player who played the highest valued trump wins
  - if no *briscole* (trumps) have been played, the player who played the highest card of the lead suit wins

Appendix 6

Unlike other trump card games, players are not required to play the same suit as the lead player.

Once the winner of a turn is determined, that player collects the played cards, and places them face down in a pile. Each player maintains his/her own pile. However, for four- and six-player versions, one player may collect all cards won by his partners. Then, each player draws a card from the remaining deck, starting with the player who won the hand, proceeding counterclockwise. The last card collected in the game is the up-turned *Briscola* card. The player who won the hand leads the next round.

People on the same team are permitted to look at each other's cards before the last hand. After all cards have been played, the total point value of cards is calculated by the individual players.

When playing in teams, partners combine their points. A variation may apply whereby the three, is ranked as a three so that a four can beat it, but the three maintains its 10-point value.

Reference: https://www.modianocards.com/learn-to-play-briscola

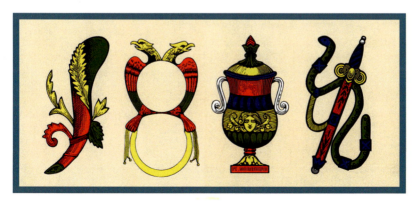

Contursi Terme — Italy